MW01035643

TECHNOLOGY, EDUCA
THE TEC SERIES

Series Editor: Marcia C. Linn
Advisory Board: Robert Bjork, Chris Dede, Joseph Krajcik, Carol Lee, Jim Minstrell, Jonathan Osborne, Mitch Resnick, Constance Steinkuehler

What's Worth Teaching?
Rethinking Curriculum in the Age of Technology
ALLAN COLLINS

Data Literacy for Educators: Making It Count in Teacher Preparation and Practice
ELLEN MANDINACH AND EDITH S. GUMMER

Assessing the Educational Data Movement
PHILIP J. PIETY

The New Science Education Leadership:
An IT-Based Learning Ecology Model
JANE F. SCHIELACK AND STEPHANIE L. KNIGHT, EDITORS

Digital Teaching Platforms:
Customizing Classroom Learning for Each Student
CHRIS DEDE AND JOHN RICHARDS, EDITORS

Leading Technology-Rich Schools:
Award-Winning Models for Success
BARBARA B. LEVIN AND LYNNE SCHRUM

The Learning Edge: What Technology Can Do to Educate All Children
ALAN BAIN AND MARK E. WESTON

Learning in the Cloud:
How (and Why) to Transform Schools with Digital Media
MARK WARSCHAUER

Video Games and Learning: Teaching and Participatory Culture in the Digital Age
KURT SQUIRE

Teaching and Learning in Public:
Professional Development Through Shared Inquiry
STEPHANIE SISK-HILTON

Rethinking Education in the Age of Technology:
The Digital Revolution and Schooling in America
ALLAN COLLINS AND RICHARD HALVERSON

The Computer Clubhouse: Constructionism and Creativity in Youth Communities
YASMIN B. KAFAI, KYLIE A. PEPPLER, AND ROBBIN N. CHAPMAN, EDITORS

WISE Science:
Web-Based Inquiry in the Classroom
JAMES D. SLOTTA AND MARCIA C. LINN

Creating and Sustaining Online Professional Learning Communities
JONI K. FALK AND BRIAN DRAYTON, EDITORS

Designing Coherent Science Education:
Implications for Curriculum, Instruction, and Policy
YAEL KALI, MARCIA C. LINN, AND JO ELLEN ROSEMAN, EDITORS

Data-Driven School Improvement:
Linking Data and Learning
ELLEN B. MANDINACH AND MARGARET HONEY, EDITORS

Electric Worlds in the Classroom: Teaching and Learning with Role-Based Computer Games
BRIAN M. SLATOR AND ASSOCIATES

Meaningful Learning Using Technology:
What Educators Need to Know and Do
ELIZABETH A. ASHBURN AND ROBERT E. FLODEN, EDITORS

WHAT'S WORTH TEACHING?

RETHINKING CURRICULUM IN THE AGE OF TECHNOLOGY

ALLAN COLLINS

Foreword by John Seely Brown

TEACHERS COLLEGE PRESS

TEACHERS COLLEGE | COLUMBIA UNIVERSITY

NEW YORK AND LONDON

Published by Teachers College Press, 1234 Amsterdam Avenue, New York, NY 10027

Copyright © 2017 by Teachers College, Columbia University

Cover by Laura Duffy Design. Photos: Wind turbines by ssuaphotos, polar bear by Yvonne Pijnenburg-Schonewille, stock data by Phongphan, researchers at table by Rawpixel.com, and cityscape by chuyuss, all via Shutterstock.

Chapter 2 contains excerpts from "The Functionality of Literacy in a Digital World," by Allan Collins and Richard Halverson, from *Reading at a Crossroads? Disjunctures and Continuities in Current Conditions and Practices,* edited by Rand J. Spiro et al. (pp. 172–179), 2015, New York, NY: Routledge. Copyright © Taylor and Francis. Reprinted by permission of the publisher.

Chapter 2 contains excerpts from "How Technology is Broadening the Nature of Learning Dialogues," by Allan Collins and Barbara Y. White, from *Socializing Intelligence Through Academic Talk and Dialogue,* edited by Lauren B. Resnick et al. (pp. 231–239), 2015, Washington, DC: AERA Books. Reprinted by permission of the publisher.

Chapter 6 contains figures adapted from "Epistemic forms and Epistemic Games: Structures and Strategies to Guide Inquiry," by Allan Collins and William Ferguson, 1993, *Educational Psychologist, 23*(1), 25–42. Copyright © Taylor and Francis. Reprinted by permission of the publisher.

Library of Congress Cataloging-in-Publication Data is available at loc.gov

ISBN 978-0-8077-5865-6 (paper)
ISBN 978-0-8077-5866-3 (hardcover)
ISBN 978-0-8077-7566-5 (ebook)

Printed on acid-free paper
Manufactured in the United States of America

24 23 22 21 20 19 18 17   8 7 6 5 4 3 2 1

To my longtime friend and colleague Barbara White, who started this work with me, but died in October 2014

CONTENTS

Foreword   John Seely Brown   ix

Acknowledgments   xi

Preface   xiii

1.   What Is Wrong with the School Curriculum?   1

Why Is the School Curriculum Full of Stuff Adults Never Use?   2

Goals of Education for a Complex Society   6

The Structure of the Book   15

2.   The New Literacy   17

The Changing Face of Literacy   18

Rethinking Education to Foster Literacy for All   22

Which Practical Literacy Skills Should Students Learn?   25

Teaching the New Literacy to All Students   32

3.   Developing Self-Sufficiency   34

The Growing Need for Self-Reliance   35

What Should Students Learn About Maintaining
   a Healthy Lifestyle?   37

What Should Students Learn About Financial
   and Legal Matters?   42

What Should Students Learn About Strategy
   and Self-Regulation?   46

Toward Schooling for Self-Reliance   53

4.   Career Skills for the New Economy   54

Learning for Tomorrow's Workplace   55

How Can Students Learn Productive Thinking?   57

How Can Students Learn to Manage Time, Resources,
   and Group-Work?   63

Building Skills Students Can Use in Future Work   69

5. **Public Policy Challenges**   **70**

Understanding Complex Systems   70

Which Environmental Issues Should Students Learn About?   72

Which Economic Issues Should Students Learn About?   76

Toward an Education for Citizens of a Global World   81

6. **Mathematical and Scientific Foundations**   **83**

Rethinking the Math and Science Curriculum   84

What Students Should Learn About Mathematical
   Foundations   85

What Students Should Learn About Scientific Foundations   92

Implications for Math and Science Education   103

7. **Passion Schools: A New Vision for School and Curriculum**   **104**

Elements of a New Vision for American Schools   105

A Vision for a 21st-Century School   111

Schools of the Future   119

References   **121**

Index   **131**

About the Author   **143**

FOREWORD

What a privilege to be asked to write a foreword for Allan Collins's newest book, *What's Worth Teaching? Rethinking Curriculum in the Age of Technology*. Both novel and revolutionary this book is. After reading it I could not help but reflect on two relevant thoughts that kept resonating in my head as I read this book. The first came from Obama's farewell speech in Chicago where he said, "Increasingly we [have] become so secure in our bubbles that we accept only information, whether true or not, that fits our opinions, instead of basing our opinions on the evidence that is out there." And the second came from David Weinberger's 2012 book *Too Big to Know*, in which he states, "We used to know how to know. We got our answers from books or experts. We'd nail down the facts and move on. We even had canons. But in the Internet age, knowledge has moved onto networks. There's more knowledge than ever, but it's different. Topics have no boundaries, and nobody agrees on anything."

This is not a bad description of our current setting, and our job as teachers, educators, designers of learning spaces, or futurists is to determine how best to educate our students, especially in K–12, to be resilient, resourceful, and inspired learners—learners who see learning as an adventure, especially so as to become lifelong learners. And from Allan's perspective this must happen early; hence rethinking our entire approach to K–12 education becomes more crucial than ever.

And Allan quickly dispels the notion that this is just a call for project-based learning. We need more. We must spend more time helping kids acquire habits of mind that help them make sense of the world through skillfully interrogating context as well as content. They don't rely on the warrants or canons that we of the postmillennial age rely on so tacitly. Interrogating context means knowing how to triangulate on sources, reading motives, questioning, unpacking evidence, and so on—and yes, kids of all ages if given the chance can acquire these skills and dispositions quite easily. As both Allan and I suggest, these skills—akin to survival skills for the networked age—can't be directly taught; they can, however, be cultivated in context.

Key here, as he shows, is that mentorship becomes increasingly important, as does peer-based learning, either face-to-face or virtual. This is how learning might be able to scale.

What I find particularly intriguing in his book is the chance to blend hand, heart, and head learning—almost a return to the mechanisms that John Dewey laid out many decades ago. Perhaps we have here a turn toward a pragmatic approach to cognition and, dare we suggest, to imagination. In a world of constant change I think we are finding that imagination is increasingly key for sense-making—reading context—and unleashing a sense of agency, from which comes identity.

Coupled with this, Allan goes on to develop the importance of each student becoming a reflective practitioner—reflecting in action and after action to see what might be learned. And what is especially powerful in scaffolding the processes of becoming a reflective practitioner is the role of collaborative sense-making. The digital age has provided many tools to make this much easier to do; now all we need is to cultivate the ability to listen to each other with a touch of humility and to engage in productive critiquing (which is different from criticism) and help instill the dispositions to do so through role modeling and skillful mentoring.

In this spirit I am intrigued by the close connection to some earlier work on how we might enable the global one-room schoolhouse, where kids learn from older kids, older kids learn how to help younger kids, and the teacher becomes a master orchestrator unleashing resources both in the room and over the network across skills, dispositions, cultures, and disciplines—where art, music, and sketching complement acquiring knowledge for knowledge's sake.

Yes, this book is a much-needed wake-up call for imaginatively rethinking what education needs to become in this complex, networked, and radically contingent world, where problems are increasingly "wicked." That is, they are not stable, are continually morphing, and are deeply entangled with each other. The problems and ideas that Allan lays out require us all to deeply rethink how we train our teachers, what schools of education need to focus on, and how we might actually create a blended epistemology, combining *homo sapiens*, *homo farber*, and *homo ludens*, enabled by focusing on an expanded appreciation and approach to imagination.

—John Seely Brown

ACKNOWLEDGMENTS

Barbara White and Charles Fadel started out as coauthors on an earlier version of the book. Barbara, in particular, helped me in writing about science and literacy. I discussed what should go into the chapters beforehand with Charles, and like Barbara, he read the chapter drafts and gave useful feedback. In negotiating with my editor, Emily Spangler, at Teachers College Press, the book changed drastically. Before that, Barbara died of cancer and Charles became engaged in other activities. So the final version of the book was largely worked out between Emily and me, with advice from my former editor, Meg Lemke, developmental editor Susan Liddicoat, and the reviewers Emily solicited for the book.

Janet Kolodner was an enormous help in preparing and editing the new final chapter. Michelle Jordan helped me edit the Preface, and John Frederiksen, who I have worked with for many years, helped draft the text on data analysis and gave me helpful feedback on statistics in the chapter on mathematical and scientific foundations. Valerie Shute suggested early on that I should emphasize systems thinking, which led to its prominence in Chapter 5. Rich Lehrer provided feedback on the chapter on mathematical and scientific foundations, and Keith Sawyer provided feedback on the section on creative thinking. Finally, Rich Halverson, my coauthor on an earlier book, *Rethinking Education in the Age of Technology*, helped draft some of the text in the new Chapter 2.

I would also like to thank the people who helped in preparing and reviewing the first draft. Longtime friends Barry Philips and Sherick Hess read most of the draft and gave me helpful, detailed comments as I went. My brother Clinton Collins read many of the chapters and gave me helpful comments on the law and justice, creative thinking, and critical thinking sections in particular. Bill Brewer took on the task of reading the whole draft, giving detailed comments at several levels on the manuscript. Shirley Brice Heath read the first eight chapters I drafted and provided wise feedback as well as specific suggestions for improving the text. Mary McCormick read the technology chapter and gave me a useful suggestion for improvement. Finally, my friend Larry Erlbaum gave me sage advice about publishers to consider.

PREFACE

In 1987, E. D. Hirsch came out with a bestselling book called *Cultural Literacy: What Every American Needs to Know*. In the Appendix is a list of more than 4,000 items labeled "What Literate Americans Know," including terms such as *antebellum, Antony's speech at Caesar's funeral*, and *atomic weight*. Later, when our family was spending the summer in San Francisco, I was reading the book to see what Hirsch had to say about the school curriculum. When we traveled by bus to various tourist sites around the city, I would read items from the Appendix to my daughter, who was 17 at the time. She would tell me what she knew about each term, and then I would tell her what I knew. During one bus ride, when a young man got off the bus, he told us, "That was the best bus ride I've ever had." It seems Hirsch was on to something.

In some sense, this book is a critique of the Hirsch book and of the many people today who are dismayed by all the things students don't know. It is an alternative view that tries to address the critical questions that Hirsch raised. He argued, "Only by accumulating shared symbols, and the shared information that the symbols represent, can we learn to communicate effectively with one another in our national community" (p. xvii). Hirsch was clearly concerned that young people were not acquiring the kind of cultural literacy he thought was required to maintain social cohesion and a literate culture. My concern is not whether students can communicate with people "in our national community," but rather whether they engage thoughtfully with important ideas and issues.

Educators need to see how the world is changing and the implications for what students should learn. Society and work are becoming ever more complex. If young people are not educated to deal with this complexity, they will have a difficult time thriving in 21st-century society. Schools everywhere are anchored in the past. They are teaching a curriculum that mostly dates back to the early 20th century, when the Carnegie Commission decided what topics should be covered in high school. Schools aren't preparing youth for the complexity of today's world. Recognizing this, elites are purchasing all sorts of educational advantages for their children outside of schools, which further accentuates the gap between the rich and poor (Collins & Halverson, 2009).

My goal in this book is to specify what a student should learn to be a knowledgeable person, a good citizen, a thoughtful worker, a reflective thinker, and a valuable friend in a complex dynamic society. For any particular job or career, there are specific kinds of knowledge one must learn. A doctor must know a lot of biology and anatomy. An accountant must know business and mathematics. I'm not trying to specify what one needs for particular occupations; people should acquire such information when they set out to pursue those careers. School often tries to inculcate knowledge that people would need in specific occupations, even when the students have no interest in pursuing those careers. I am trying to specify what is important to learn no matter what career one may choose.

I believe, like George Washington and Thomas Jefferson before me, that people must be educated to make wise policy decisions. As Washington argued, "In proportion as the structure of government gives force to public opinion, it is essential that public opinion be enlightened" (quoted in Cremin, 1951, p. 29). And Jefferson wrote to his friend George Wythe, "Preach, my dear sir, a crusade against ignorance; establish and improve the law for educating the common people. Let our countrymen know . . . that the tax which will be paid for this purpose is not more than the thousandth part of what will be paid to kings, priests and nobles who will rise up among us if we leave the people in ignorance" (quoted in Cremin, 1980, p. 108). Given the complexity of living today, making wise public policy decisions requires substantial understanding of topics such as economics, health, law, and the environment.

Digital technologies are changing every aspect of life. As the rate of invention and innovation increases, we need to learn to cope with the uncertainty that permeates our experience of novelty, unpredictability, and change. This book discusses the kind of knowledge young people need to thrive in a complex and changing world. They need to see the trends that are shaping the world and deal with uncertainty through experimentation, creativity, and improvisation. They need to critically evaluate their options to make good decisions about their lives. They need to navigate through complex legal and political systems. They need the understanding to make wise decisions about the environment, the economy, and their health. They need to work productively with people from other cultures on the common problems to be faced. All this requires a different kind of knowledge from what school is offering today.

In summary, I am attempting to specify what knowledge is most useful in the current world, based on the knowledge humanity has accumulated over the years. I've acquired a large amount of knowledge that is, at best, marginal to my existence, needed only to solve crossword puzzles, play Trivial Pursuit, or regale bus riders in San Francisco. My decisions about what is worth learning are based on long experience as well as the study of education, science, and mathematics. I surely will omit important ideas and include things that are somewhat marginal to living in the current milieu. But the main purpose of the book is to raise the issue of deciding what is worth learning.

We educators can't go on adding things to the school curriculum as knowledge grows exponentially. We can't keep people in school longer and longer, until everyone needs several advanced degrees just to deal with the complexity they face in their lives. We can't make our textbooks much fatter than they already are and cover more and more topics in the same amount of time. We can't keep students in school 12 hours a day and 12 months of the year. Our strategies for coping with the exponential growth of knowledge are hitting a wall.

In this book, I zoom through a lot of different topics. My explanations are inevitably oversimplified, but I hope to capture the essence of ideas that are helpful for young people to understand. Some of what I say may be incorrect or incomplete, but that is not the point of the book. I'm trying to say which ideas are worth learning, given the trends that are occurring in our world. This is clearly an impossible task. What I get wrong, others can correct. What I leave out, others can fill in. But I need to be specific enough to get the conversation started about what really is useful.

I don't think the ideas I discuss in the book are requirements that every student must learn. Instead, they are representative of the kinds of knowledge, skills, and dispositions I think are critical for thriving in a complex world. A longer version of the book would describe other topics I think are important, such as trends in history (for example, the decline of violence), risk analysis, cultural evolution, engineering, and design. I simply don't believe in requirements. I think all students should pursue deep knowledge about the things they care about. The trick is to design the school curriculum in such a way that the important things to learn are embedded in topics that students care about. The final chapter addresses this issue.

It is time for educators to rethink what is critical to learn in a complex and changing society. This involves different knowledge from what schools are teaching. In a world where technology is usurping routine work and affecting every aspect of our lives, learning and thinking have become central to leading a productive life. Schools will have to make radical changes if they hope to prepare students for the rapidly changing world they are entering.

CHAPTER 1

WHAT IS WRONG WITH
THE SCHOOL CURRICULUM?

In the movie *Peggy Sue Got Married* (Gurian & Coppola, 1986), a middle-aged Peggy Sue tries to forget her marital problems with her husband, Charlie, by renewing old friendships at her 25th high school class reunion. Wondering if she made the right decisions in her life, Peggy Sue gets a chance to try again when, zapped into a time warp, she finds herself a teenager back in 1960. Thrust back into algebra class, she faces a test, which she turns in blank to her teacher. She explains her failure with the following quote: "Well, Mr. Snelgrove, I happen to know that in the future I will not have the slightest use for algebra, and I speak from experience."

Peggy Sue's problem with algebra is pervasive throughout the school curriculum. Most students see no reason why they should learn about factoring polynomials and parsing sentences and the Holy Roman Empire and stomata when they cannot imagine that this information will be of any use to them later in life. And for the most part they are right. The school curriculum is filled with stuff that most people will never use, and hence will forget as soon as they leave school or move on to the next grade.

There is ample evidence that students do not remember most of what they are taught in school. Philip Sadler (1987) found that when he asked Harvard seniors at graduation, "What causes the phases of the moon?" only 3 out of 24 knew the correct answer. And when he asked, "What causes the seasons?" only 1 in 24 knew the correct answer, even though these ideas were taught in elementary or middle school.[1] Similarly, studies have found that only a

---

1. Most adults in America think the phases of the moon are caused by the shadow of the Earth. In fact, the phases are caused by the spatial relation between the sun and moon as seen from Earth. As the moon goes around Earth, when the moon is in the direction of the sun, we see a new moon, and when it is in the opposite direction from the sun, we see a full moon. Similarly, most adults in America think the seasons are caused by changes in the distance of Earth from the sun. Actually, the seasons are caused by the angle of the sun's rays as they hit Earth. Earth is tilted in its orbit as it goes around the sun, and so in our winter (in the Northern Hemisphere), the direct rays fall on the Southern Hemisphere and in our summer, they fall on the Northern Hemisphere.

1

third of adults know how to convert between systems of measurement and calculate with mixed units, such as hours and minutes (Packer, 1997). Nor can most adults add and multiply fractions, or remember when the French Revolution occurred. These are all facts and procedures that they learned in school, but with no reason to use the knowledge, most forget that they ever learned these things. It is time to ask if what educators are teaching is the best use of school time.

I'm not arguing that it is unimportant to know science, mathematics, history, geography, literature, and the arts. These are the centerpieces of the school curriculum, and they are more important than ever for living in a complex society. The problem is with the specific content of what school is teaching in these domains and what it is leaving out. What is left out, such as social intelligence and strategic thinking, goes much beyond the standard disciplines covered in school.

WHY IS THE SCHOOL CURRICULUM FULL OF STUFF ADULTS NEVER USE?

In his book *Cultural Literacy*, E. D. Hirsch (1987) decried the fact that students didn't know when World Wars I and II occurred, where Toronto is, and who Thomas Jefferson was. In fact, he makes reference to the large amount of literature that documents all the kinds of things students don't know. Of course, for the most part, their parents didn't know these things either, unless they happened to have lived through the events. Nor should we suppose, as Hirsch does, that students used to know these things and don't anymore. As Sam Weinberg (2004) points out, when you look at history tests going back to 1917, "today's high school students do about as well as their parents, grandparents, and great-grandparents" (p. 1406). There is evidence from IQ tests administered over many years that people have been scoring better at a rate of 3% each decade (Flynn, 1999). If anything, people are getting "smarter." The concern that many express about the failure to remember what they think are basic facts about the world is but one symptom of what is wrong with the school curriculum.

Inclusion of Topics

The country is teeming with people who want to make sure that their favorite facts and skills get into the school curriculum. Biologists want us to know about stomata, and historians about the French Revolution. Conservatives want us to know about Ronald Reagan, and liberals, about Franklin Roosevelt. Recently, conservatives on the Texas School Board voted to require students to learn about the roles of Phyllis Schlafly, the Contract with America, the Heritage Foundation, the Moral Majority, and the National Rifle Association (Brick, 2010). Although this may serve the board's conservative agenda, these are not the kind of powerful ideas that will make students productive citizens.

In connection with the Third International Mathematics and Science Study (TIMSS), Gilbert Valverde and William Schmidt (1997) reported that American 4th-grade students perform near the top in comparison with students in other countries, but by 8th grade, they perform below average. They found that when compared to the top-performing countries, U.S. textbooks in math and science are much heavier and the number of topics covered much greater. They explain the poor performance of American students in the following terms: "This is true because breadth of topics is presented in these textbooks at the expense of depth of coverage. Consequently, our textbooks are limited to perfunctory treatment of subject matter" (p. 65). I think the excess of topics covered in American textbooks reflects the demand by different interest groups to include their favorite topics in the curriculum. Few seem to be asking which topics are really worth including. This is why the American curriculum is "a mile wide and an inch deep."

Inheritance from the Past

Raymond Callahan (1962) wrote a classic book in which he described how the institution of schooling developed in an earlier time to take on many of the trappings of an industrial factory. There is a mass-production character to the way knowledge is poured into students at each grade, and they are moved along the production line until they come out at the end with a high school diploma. Alternatively, they are thrown away as rejects before they finish. In many large cities in America, a high proportion of the students who start school in 1st grade never receive a high school diploma.

Alvin Toffler (1980) refers to the "covert curriculum" as emphasizing punctuality, obedience, and rote repetitive work. As Toffler argues, "Factory labor demanded workers who showed up on time, especially assembly-line hands. It demanded workers who would take orders from a management hierarchy without questioning. And it demanded men and women prepared to slave away at machines or in offices, performing brutally repetitious operations" (p. 29). Our current model of universal schooling is an Industrial Age institution, and it is not at all clear how well it can adapt to the Information Age, where thinking and creativity are prized.

Another problem is that the structure of the school curriculum was inherited from the 19th century and before. Though a few topics have dropped out of the standard curriculum, such as Greek and Latin, calculating square roots, and carrying out mathematical proofs, most of the 19th-century curriculum is still there, along with the addition of new topics as knowledge accumulates. At the same time, computer technology is changing what is worth learning. Computers can carry out all the mathematical algorithms that are taught to students up through graduate school, yet much of the math curriculum still centers on teaching students to carry out algorithms. Understanding mathematical ideas is more important than ever, and yet math education is focused on teaching students to simulate what computers do much more effectively than people ever will.

The Internet is a gigantic memory storage device with easy access from smartphones. If you want to know who Thomas Jefferson is, where Toronto is, or when the French Revolution occurred, you can easily find the answers on the web. So why is it important for people to know these facts? You can argue, as Hirsch does, that in order to carry on intelligent conversations with other people, you must have these kinds of facts at your fingertips. But these are not the kinds of topics that come up in most people's conversations. And if they come up in reading, they can easily be accessed. I would argue that this kind of knowledge does not give people the ability to make sense of the world around them and function well in it. So why is an enormous amount of time spent teaching these kinds of facts when most of them will be forgotten? Until educators design schools that let students pursue ideas they care about at their own pace, students are bound to forget most of what they learn in school.

Influence of Testing

In his book *Mindstorms: Children, Computers, and Powerful Ideas*, Seymour Papert (1980) argues that you have to love ideas to reach deep understanding of the world. Yet school does not foster a love of learning. Some people do come to love learning in spite of school, but school tends to eliminate the romance of ideas, because the goal is to make sure everyone learns what experts have decided is important. School does not let kids pursue their passions. Rather, school breaks topics down into small units and keeps moving from topic to topic to make sure everything is covered. There is no time to stop and smell the roses. The next test is coming soon.

Papert (1980) goes on to argue:

> Skills and discrete facts are easy to give out in controlled doses. They are easier to measure. And it is certainly easier to enforce the learning of a skill than it is to check whether someone "has gotten to know" an idea. It is not surprising that schools emphasize learning skills and facts and that students pick up an image of learning as "learning that" and "learning how." (p. 136)

As Papert suggested more than 35 years ago, testing has had a strong, often subtle, influence over the school curriculum. A major goal of educational testing has been to develop objective tests that cover the wide scope of topics taught in schools. This forces the construction of tests with a large number of questions that require closed-form answers, such as selecting from multiple-choice items. Philip Piety (2013) and Vicki Abeles (2015) show how these types of tests lead to widespread cheating and teaching to the test.

To construct such tests, educators break down what it takes to accomplish complex tasks into a set of facts and skills that can be measured with short items. A good example of the perversion this leads to comes from the way writing ability used to be tested. Because writing involves producing multiple paragraphs of text, there was no way to score it objectively. Therefore, assessment of writing used to be based on vocabulary items, grammar items, and editing items, all of which could be scored objectively. Finally, the writing community rebelled against this strategy and insisted that the only way to evaluate writing was to have students write. Then educators developed rubrics (i.e., standards) for scoring short essays and training for scorers that would produce reliable scoring that was considered objective. Still, English teachers who score such tests feel the scoring rubrics and methods are a kind of straitjacket. Creativity and development of complex arguments do not come into current writing evaluation. But current writing assessments are certainly much better than grammar items and editing tasks.

The problem of assessing a complex task like writing illustrates the way assessment has distorted what we teach in school. There are many complex capabilities that objective-assessment techniques have no way to measure. They are the kind of capabilities that are critical for addressing the ill-structured and ambiguous challenges life throws at us. Some of the most important goals of education have been deemphasized because of school's emphasis on easy-to-score tests. They include the following:

- Solving complex problems that actually arise in the world
- Making persuasive presentations and arguments orally
- Finding and researching questions that are worth pursuing
- Figuring out what is going on in some complex situation and being able to diagnose problems with the process
- Designing artifacts and systems to accomplish meaningful goals
- Taking responsibility for completing a substantial piece of work
- Listening to what other people are saying and being able to make sense of different viewpoints
- Asking facilitative questions of other people and getting them to think about what they are doing

- Evaluating sources of information as to how credible they are
- Understanding deeply several domains of inquiry of particular interest, such as environmental issues, political history, or literary theory
- Reading materials that relate to students' interests and goals
- Working well with others to plan and carry out tasks
- Making important decisions, such as what career to pursue and how to keep the body physically fit

These goals strike me as very different from the kinds of goals that are embodied in the tests that we are using to make schools more accountable.

With the increased emphasis on testing in schools, the curriculum has been steadily narrowing over many years to focus on facts and skills that are easily measured. This means that school is preparing young people less and less well for the kinds of thinking careers that will pay a living wage in the 21st century.

GOALS OF EDUCATION FOR A COMPLEX SOCIETY

In order to say what is worth learning, we need to think about the central goals of education. Different people and societies have diverse goals, and these goals change over time as societies evolve. The needs of people living today are very different from the goals of educators who put together the school curriculum in the 19th and 20th centuries, most of which have no relation to the needs of young people today.

David Cohen (Powell, Farrar, & Cohen, 1985) addressed educational priorities in the following terms:

> Americans will never completely agree on educational purposes. . . . They might have decided for instance that their chief purpose was to produce students who could read well and critically, who could write plainly and persuasively, and who could reason clearly. Reading, writing, and reasoning are not subjects— they are intellectual capacities. They can be taught by studying academic disciplines, but only if the teachers possess the capacities in good measure, if they are trying to teach those capacities rather than to cover the material, and if the materials for study are arranged so as to cultivate those capacities—as opposed, say, to the capacity to remember a few facts, or write down disjointed bits of information. (p. 306)

In 2009, I asked Northwestern University graduate students in a course on the history of education to formulate a curriculum for the American high school. The students decided to organize the curriculum around four areas derived from Cohen and his colleague's suggestion:

1. Reading and thinking critically
2. Communicating effectively in different media
3. Reasoning logically in different domains
4. Carrying out investigations about diverse issues

Their plan would have the topics from different disciplines, such as English, history, mathematics, science, and the arts, embedded in each of the four areas. They felt that such a curriculum could move education away from its focus on facts and skills to building the kind of intellectual capacities needed for living in the 21st century.

In 1991, the U.S. Labor Department published the Secretary's Commission on Achieving Necessary Skills (SCANS) report (SCANS Commission, 1991), in which it tried to specify the kinds of generic knowledge and capabilities that would be needed for careers in the 21st century. The report argued that learners should be educated in five areas called core competencies:

1. Identifying, organizing, planning, and allocating resources
2. Working with others
3. Acquiring and using information
4. Understanding complex systems
5. Working with a variety of technologies

The report argued that these new competencies should be built upon a foundation of basic skills, thinking skills, and interpersonal qualities, such as responsibility and integrity. The SCANS report is a symptom of the changing demands on education needed for complex jobs. Over the past century, routine jobs have been disappearing, and the demand for flexibility and thinking has grown. People will have to keep learning new knowledge and skills throughout their lifetimes, as their lives and jobs keep changing.

Since the SCANS report, a large number of books and reports have addressed the kinds of knowledge and skills that will be needed for careers in the future. For example, in his book *The Global Achievement Gap*, Tony Wagner (2008) specifies seven survival skills that he feels are critical for dealing with an increasingly competitive world:

1. Critical thinking and problem solving
2. Collaboration across networks and leading by influence
3. Agility and adaptability

4. Initiative and entrepreneurialism
5. Effective oral and written communication
6. Accessing and analyzing information
7. Curiosity and imagination

These seven emphasize the kind of soft skills that are rarely taught in school.

Similarly, in their book *21st Century Skills: Learning for Life in Our Times*, Bernie Trilling and Charles Fadel (2009) argue that the capabilities people need fall into three categories:

1. Learning and innovation skills, such as critical thinking and problem solving
2. Digital literacy skills, such as information and media literacy
3. Career and life skills, such as adaptability and self-direction

These three categories nicely encompass most of the kinds of capabilities that recent books and reports are advocating.

Although I support these arguments for the new kinds of capabilities that are necessary for living in the 21st century, I take a somewhat broader approach in trying to identify critical ideas, strategies, and dispositions that are important to cultivate. These reports focus on career skills, whereas I also want to identify ideas, strategies, and dispositions that are critical to making wise personal and policy decisions, and to living a productive and satisfying life.

Different Kinds of Powerful Ideas

My argument is that school has failed to focus on the kinds of powerful ideas that will make students smarter. These powerful ideas come in many varieties. There are competencies such as those suggested by David Cohen and colleagues (1985). There are beliefs and dispositions that are important, such as persistence and love of learning. There are strategies for dealing with problems, learning about new topics, and inventing new solutions and ideas. There are ideas with wide applicability that are critical for understanding the world. There are frameworks that help people organize knowledge and access it when needed. There are distinctions that are critical for making effective decisions. All of this is the kind of knowledge on which schools need to focus.

Competencies. Consider the four competencies suggested by the Northwestern students' curriculum. *Reading and thinking critically* involves not simply interpreting text, but also interpreting and evaluating tables, figures, oral discourse, graphs, animations, videos, simulations, and all the other media that now pervade our lives. *Communicating effectively in different media* involves making videos and presentations, listening to others, constructing digital representations of yourself and your ideas, and using new media to make effective arguments and negotiate with other people. *Reasoning logically in different domains* requires much more than mathematical and scientific reasoning. It requires understanding how other people may reason or react to different events, considering how different situations may develop and anticipating how to respond to them, making analogies and evaluating their strengths and limitations, and projecting trends and possible scenarios into the future. *Carrying out investigations about diverse issues* may involve historical, mathematical, legal, medical, and other issues that come up in life. There are surely other competencies that are important to success in life, but these four are certainly critical.

Beliefs and dispositions. Perhaps the most important thing a learner can acquire is a productive set of beliefs and dispositions. Though some dispositions are inborn, most are acquired, and even inborn dispositions can be modified with experience. One approach to teaching dispositions was developed at the Central Park East Secondary School in Harlem, New York (Darling-Hammond, Ancess, & Falk, 1995; Meier, 1995). The school stressed that students should learn to ask and answer reflective questions that correspond to five Habits of Mind:

1. From what viewpoint are we seeing, reading, or hearing this?
2. How do we know what we know? What's the evidence, and how reliable is it?
3. How are things, events, or people connected? What is the cause and effect? How do they fit?
4. What if . . . ? Could things be otherwise? What are or were the alternatives?
5. So what? Why does it matter? What does it all mean? Who cares?

Students were encouraged to develop a disposition to ask themselves these questions as they went through the school, because the questions were central to everything they did in the school. And the students had to answer these questions about their work in oral and written exams to determine if they learned enough to graduate. These questions stretch the definition of what is taught in a school to encompass the types of dispositions required for adaptive thinking in an information-rich world.

Beyond the kinds of dispositions taught in the Harlem high school, many different beliefs and dispositions are critical to living well—important beliefs, for example, that you can accomplish most tasks if you work at them, and that you should focus your efforts on tasks that are worthwhile and will make the most contribution to the world. There are social beliefs, such as that most people try to be helpful and that cooperation is critical to accomplishing most goals. There are social dispositions, such as showing interest in others' ideas and listening carefully when they tell you things, helping others and not making a lot of demands on them in return, and trying to understand where other people are coming from. There are dispositions that embody important capabilities, such as planning what you are going to do before you do it, monitoring your progress as you work and checking it afterward, and reflecting on how your work might be improved.

Strategies. Strategies for successful living are often linked to productive dispositions. For example, one strategy for effective listening is to take others' ideas and elaborate or summarize them, perhaps improving the ideas in the process. Another strategy is to admit your own errors when you discover them, so that other people will take your ideas seriously. Developing strategies like these for working with other people is critical to productivity. Equally critical are strategies for planning, monitoring, and reflecting on your own work. For example, an effective strategy for reflecting is to identify a set of criteria for evaluating your work before you start and then apply the criteria as you proceed and when you finish (White & Frederiksen, 1998). In this book, I discuss a wide variety of strategies for critical thinking, carrying out investigations, and creating ideas and products.

Ideas with wide applicability. In his book *The Children's Machine*, Seymour Papert (1997) discusses the importance of the idea of modularity. Modularity describes the way that systems are broken down into subsystems, which function fairly autonomously from one another. So, for example, the human body has subsystems such as the nervous system and the circulatory system, and cars have subsystems, such as the propulsion system and the electrical system. Papert points out how important modularity is to debugging computer programs, because problems can be isolated to different subsystems, which reduces the search space for finding the problem. Modularity is equally important in troubleshooting electrical systems. In his book *The Sciences of the Artificial*, Herbert Simon (1969), a winner of the Nobel Prize, explains how modularity is critical in designing systems because it frees the designer to design and modify each subsystem somewhat independently of the other subsystems. The idea of modularity has very wide applicability in both natural and artificial systems. It is critical to designing systems and to figuring out what is wrong with systems when they are not functioning properly.

Similarly, the idea of incentives in economics has wide applicability. One economist likes to introduce students to the field of economics with a story about how the British used to ship criminals to Australia. Many of the prisoners would die during the ocean trip. These deaths caused outrage among the British public, but none of the measures they tried, such as putting doctors onboard the ships, could fix the problem. Finally, an economist suggested that they pay the ship captains based on the number of healthy prisoners who arrived in Australia, rather than the number deported, and the problem fixed itself. Understanding how incentives work has huge implications for both personal and policy decisions in a complex society.

Domain frameworks. A domain framework is a structure that organizes a whole field of inquiry, such as economics or biology. In conducting a study where I asked scientists to explain why American wages had fallen in real terms between the early 1970s and the early 1990s, all the respondents accounted for the drop in terms of factors that affect supply and demand (Collins, 2011). Supply and demand is a central framework in the field of economics, and to understand it properly, you need to know how different variables affect it. Supply and demand is critical to understanding much of what goes on in the financial world around us. Similarly, understanding evolution is critical to understanding much of what happens in biology and the environment. In addition, evolution is a generative idea that has given rise to other robust ideas, such as memes (Dawkins, 1976). As defined on Wikipedia, "a meme is an idea, behavior, or style that spreads from person to person within a culture," much like genes spread biological information. Domain frameworks, like evolution or supply and demand, help organize whole fields of knowledge, and so they are critical to remembering and finding the information needed to make sense of the world.

Critical distinctions. Some critical distinctions are taught in schools, such as between creative, persuasive, and descriptive writing, or between solids, liquids, and gases. But there are many critical distinctions that are not taught, such as between the different kinds of governments and the different kinds of enterprises. For example, there are critical distinctions between public corporations, family-owned businesses, partnerships, cooperatives, and nonprofits that are important to understand, both from a policy and a personal perspective. In the chapters that follow, I emphasize a number of critical distinctions, along with what people should understand about these distinctions.

Distinguishing What Is Worth Learning
from What Is Not Worth Learning

As I argued earlier, much of what is taught in school is not particularly important to learn, unless a young person goes into a career where that particular knowledge is needed. How can we distinguish what is worth learning from what is not? The answers I offer may upset a lot of people who are invested in what is currently taught in school.

Because the Internet is becoming a storehouse of all the world's knowledge, it is less and less important today to know a lot of facts. For example, knowledge such as dates and places have become less important. But that raises the question of how people can learn about historical trends, if they do not learn the dates when critical events happened. And it raises the further question of how people can understand the world if they do not know the names of places around the world. Let me address these two questions.

Because most people do not use dates in their normal activities, most people are going to forget them. I think a better way to learn about historical trends is to understand different eras in history and the approximate time periods when these eras occurred. To take Western history as an example, it can be broken into the eras of the hunter-gatherer societies; the early empires in Sumer, Egypt, Greece, and Rome; the Middle Ages and feudal society; the Renaissance; the Age of Exploration; the Reformation; the Enlightenment; the Industrial Revolution; and the Modern Era. Although a few dates, like 1492, might be memorable, the rest are not worth teaching because nothing depends on them. It is the trends of history that are important.

In teaching geography, schools emphasize a lot of information that is useless to most people, such as the capitals and regions of different countries. This, again, is information that will not make any difference in most people's lives, and it takes time away from much more important things, such as the basic history and location of major countries, including Britain, France, Germany, China, India, Japan, and Russia, and for Americans, Mexico and Canada. There are many countries and places that most people will never remember unless those countries happen to become tangled up in current events. At that time, people may want to learn more about those places and can turn to the web for information, but it is not worthwhile to spend time on a lot of places that are unlikely to be important to most people's lives. It would be better, instead, to understand the culture, economies, and geopolitics of important countries and their relations to one another.

Although I do not discuss in the book what students should learn about how government functions, I do think schools that engage students in legislative simulations provide useful knowledge that helps students understand the kinds of trade-offs central to running an effective government. I also think it would be useful for students to investigate the pros and cons of different governance systems, such as presidential systems, parliamentary systems, and corporate systems. Understanding how governance systems function is important to becoming a good citizen at the local, national, and international level.

Because computers can carry out all the algorithms that are taught in school up through graduate school, one might argue that knowing the multiplication table has become less important when there are calculators in our smartphones and computers. But knowing the multiplication table may, in fact, be critical to making estimations, such as estimating the cost of a carpet for your living room if it sells for eight dollars a square yard. If estimates involving multiplication are frequent, it may remain critical to learn the multiplication table at a young age, unless everyone has a smartphone at the ready. Estimating is a critical skill in monitoring your work on problems and in evaluating your work when you are done. These strategic skills are crucial in everything one does.

To illustrate the importance of estimation and reasoning, the school superintendent in Manchester, New Hampshire, in the 1930s had his teachers give up teaching math algorithms for the first 5 years of school, and instead focus on math reasoning and estimation tasks (Benezet, 1991). He was provoked to make this change when he asked students problems such as "If half a stick is buried in mud at the bottom of a pond, two-thirds of the rest is in the water, and 1 foot is above water, how long is the stick?" Students who were taught in the traditional manner would start adding the numbers given (1/2+2/3+1), whereas the students taught in the new manner would reason through the problem. His revision of the curriculum opted for thoughtfulness over memorization of algorithms, but of course, it didn't last after he retired.

There are a large number of problem types taught in math and science courses that teach procedures that people will never use, unless they enter particular professions. For example, in algebra courses, students are often taught to solve flow-rate problems, such as "If it takes one pump 4 hours to fill a swimming pool, and another pump 3 hours, how long will it take for both pumps to fill the pool?" Like most story problems in math, this is a problem that no one is ever likely to face, as Peggy Sue pointed out to her algebra teacher. It is no wonder that most people forget most of what they are taught in math and science classes.

One of the major curriculum arguments concerns whether there are great works of literature, known as the canon, that everyone should read. I would argue that it is important for people to read extensively, but there is no one body of work that everyone should read. Forcing everyone to read Shakespeare, for example, produces a lot of people who hate Shakespeare.

This is counterproductive. Ideally, students would read deeply in areas they care about, whether it be military history, poetry, English novels, science fiction, mystery stories, or mechanics. One might need guidance to find readings that promote deep knowledge about a topic, but teachers, networks of friends who are interested in similar topics, or even computer systems can make good recommendations. Pursuing topics deeply has much more payoff in a complex society than having a smattering of knowledge about many different topics, such as I have.

If schools encouraged students to read about things they care about, rather than the things that are "good for them," I think students would do a lot more reading. They could participate in groups, in class or online, with other students having similar interests, where they discuss what they read. They could write critical reviews of what they read. The problem is that the modern school, unlike the one-room schoolhouse of the past, is built on the idea of the whole class doing the same thing at the same time. Encouraging students to pursue topics they care about is regarded as something they can do outside of school.

As for foreign languages, I think for most American students, the time spent learning languages is wasted. I studied Latin, French, and German over the years, and none of it has done me any particular good, except for working crossword puzzles. In fact, soon people will have access to smartphones that can translate from one language to another for them. Of course, students who are interested in languages should study those languages that they care about, but forcing American students to study foreign languages is not a good use of their time. This is not particularly true of Europeans, who interact much more frequently with people from other countries and where the lingua franca is English. It obviously benefits most people around the world to be able to speak English, but other languages not so much.

With respects to the arts, I think that schools should encourage students to pursue deeply those arts they care most about. This is the approach taken in the Digital Youth Network (Barron, Gomez, Pinkard, & Martin, 2014) and Central Park East Secondary School (Darling-Hammond, Ancess, & Falk, 1995), as described in Chapters 2 and 7. The Internet has expanded the range of arts people can easily produce and display, such as creating online games, music videos, digital art, or fan fiction. And as Steve Jobs taught us, an artistic sense of design is often critical to the success of new products. Young people can now produce their work on the web for display and possible sale to the world. The Internet, indeed, may bring about a renaissance in artistic production.

Schools often set up requirements for students to learn things they will never use in later life. That is the moral of Peggy Sue's story. In a world where kids can pursue whatever interests them on the Internet, schools must learn to be more careful about what they require students to learn. Otherwise, they will find themselves with more rebellious students, many of whom will tune out or drop out. It is a mantra of adult education that you can't teach adults anything they don't think they need or want to learn. Our kids have been "adultified" by the modern world, as Neil Postman (1982, 1985) has pointed out in his books. Schools will do well to reduce their requirements and instead encourage students to learn what they care about most.

THE STRUCTURE OF THE BOOK

How must schools adapt to the 21st century? The book is organized around five trends that have deep implications for what schools should be teaching:

- *Chapter 2.* In the youth culture of today, children as young as 6 are texting their friends, setting up Facebook pages, and joining fan fiction clubs and other web communities, all of which have deep implications for the teaching of literacy and social skills.
- *Chapter 3.* As society evolves toward more independent living and working (what is being called the "gig economy"), people must become more self-sufficient. This requires that they understand complex issues of health, law, and finance and exercise self-control over their lives and decisions.
- *Chapter 4.* As technology has become more pervasive, the demand for workers who can do routine jobs has decreased in favor of workers who can think critically and creatively to solve problems, manage their time and resources, and work productively with other people.
- *Chapter 5.* Society is facing increasingly complex policy challenges that require greater public understanding, such as climate change, pollution, public health, immigration, and government financing. In order to make wise policy decisions, citizens must become much better informed about the complex trade-offs involved in these policies.
- *Chapter 6.* The foundations of mathematics and science have become critical to everything we do in a complex society. They are the basis for most of the inventions and innovations that are critical to a growing economy. In simpler times, before the Industrial Revolution, people did not need deep understanding of mathematics and science to make wise public and personal decisions, but as the complexity of the world has increased, these decisions have grown ever more difficult.

Chapter 7 concludes the book with a vision of how to reconstitute school and curriculum to better address the changing demands of society. My vision incorporates important principles for the redesign of schooling to make the teaching and learning more appropriate for developing the skills and knowledge that will be needed in the 21st century. It embodies authentic tasks and assessments, a dual focus on the teaching of particular competencies in the context of accomplishing meaningful tasks, peer teaching and mentoring, and a learning cycle of planning, doing, and reflecting. The goal is to develop schooling that will have a major impact on student motivation and learning, and will better prepare students for the complex world they are entering.

My main purpose in this book is to raise the question of what is worth teaching, not to insist that I know the right answers. Up to now, the process by which topics get into the school curriculum has not been based on a consideration of the most useful kinds of knowledge for people living in a complex and changing society. It is time for society to debate what is worth teaching. The concrete suggestions in the following chapters are meant to start this debate.

CHAPTER 2

THE NEW LITERACY

As Cynthia Lewis (2007) argues in the book *A New Literacies Sampler*, "New technologies afford new practices, but it is the practices themselves, and the local and global contexts within which they are situated, that are central to new literacies. The logical implication . . . is that schools would accomplish more if, like new literacy users, they too focused on practices rather than tools. . . . Through professional development, teachers receive training in curricular uses of technology, but they do not learn about new mindsets, identities, and practices that come with new technologies, forms of communication, and economic flows" (p. 230).

Children are spending increasing amounts of time communicating in different ways using new digital technologies. Children are texting their friends; setting up Facebook pages to interact with others; playing online games where they read about strategy and communicate with other players; spending time at websites like Webkinz World, Club Penguin, and Barbie Girls; and joining fan fiction clubs and other web communities where people of different ages pursue their interests. These activities are changing the face of literacy.

They provide a variety of new incentives for kids to read and write. Their accessibility "anytime, anywhere" and the ability to broadly publish with the touch of a finger uniquely develops children's identities as literate people who are empowered to interact with the world. This is a radically different world from the one in which most of us grew up. It behooves literacy educators to incorporate the power of these activities into the ways we teach literacy, as Cynthia Lewis advocates above.

In 21st-century communication, the boundaries between core literacy practices, such as learning to read and write, and more applied production and presentation practices are becoming blurred. Creating multimedia documents, putting together and critiquing videos, finding information and resources on the web, and understanding images and graphics are all becoming important aspects of communication.

New technologies offer interesting ways to make the transition between basic and applied literacies. For example, people who play massively multiplayer online games use basic literacy practices to develop a whole range of skills, such as persuasion, negotiation, forming alliances, strategizing, outwitting opponents, calculating which approach is most likely to work, and communicating with different kinds of people. These literacy skills are critical to functioning in the high-tech culture that is developing around us. Schools need to find a way to use technology to engage students in developing the new literacies that are critical to functioning in today's world.

THE CHANGING FACE OF LITERACY[1]

When young children learn to listen and talk, they are driven by the desire to get their parents to respond to their desires. Learning to understand what their parents are saying and learning to tell their parents what they want has a huge payoff for young kids. Not so for learning to read and write in school. Traditionally, by learning to read and write, kids gained very little ability to control the world around them, unlike what they gained by learning to listen and talk. The major payoff for learning to read and write in kids' eyes has been to please parents and teachers. If their parents and teachers didn't much care, then there was very little incentive for kids to learn to read and write.

Student work in schools has always faced the artificial barrier of being legitimate solely within the confines of the classroom. When only teachers see student work, students do not experience the authentic feedback that results from exposing their work to a real audience. In the case of initially learning a subject, insulating their learning from external critique may make sense. But as their work matures, students need opportunities to demonstrate their learning in legitimate contexts outside the classroom. The development of the Internet makes it possible for student work to become much more widely available to the rest of the world. The web is the first mass medium that has open access, allowing anyone to publish their work in a place that potentially has a worldwide audience. This can provide a powerful motivation for students to produce substantial works that are meaningful to the community.

The Internet offers many venues for communicating with the world. Students can send emails to other students and adults around the world. They can participate in chat rooms and communities that have participants from many different locations. A main motivation for participation in social networking sites is the opportunity to publish a representation of yourself

---

1. The next two sections are based on Collins and Halverson (2015).

that others will see. Constructing representations of your thoughts, preferences, and creativity allows others to identify you as a possible friend, or can open you up to criticism from those who do not share your tastes. In either case, participants learn about what they really think, and gain self-awareness from publishing public representations of themselves. These different venues provide a reason to communicate with different kinds of people, and so they provide a meaningful purpose for reading, writing, and developing multimedia presentations.

Computer environments such as multi-user virtual environments (MUVEs) allow people from all over the world to converse by typing while they explore places that others have created for them. Some of these MUVEs, such as Moose Crossing, designed by Amy Bruckman (2000), have been created particularly for children. In Moose Crossing, children are creating a virtual world out of words, making magical places and creatures that have behaviors. In the process, they are improving their reading and creative writing skills, and learning how to write computer programs.

Often in such MUVEs the more experienced are mentoring the less experienced—learning more deeply by teaching. For example, Bruckman (2000) describes how 13-year-old Rachael mentored a 12-year-old girl named Storm in how to use the system. When Rachael saw that Storm had joined Moose Crossing, she sent a message to offer help and show her around. Rachael provided examples of pets, which Storm could use to create her own pets. Rachael looked at Storm's code to help her debug the problems she was having. She took her to play in the clouds and build a home on Paradise Island. She provided moral support when Storm had trouble creating a mouse for her cat to play with. By the end of the weekend, Storm was, in turn, supporting Rachael in spelling and debugging her own programs. And in the process, both were improving their reading and creative writing skills, as well as learning how to write computer programs. This new type of technology-based learning environment facilitates peer mentoring, which has been shown to be a powerful learning technique (Heath & Mangiola, 1991).

The interactivity of new media technologies provides a number of capabilities that can enhance education. As is evident from the popularity of computer games, interactivity can be very engaging. Interaction also allows learners to see the consequences of their actions. In this way, they have their expectations and predictions confirmed or disconfirmed, and can try different courses of action to evaluate their relative effectiveness. Colette Daiute (1985) demonstrates that children using word processors write better essays, because they can read their typed words, whereas they cannot easily read their own handwriting. Hence, they get immediate feedback on how they are doing, which they can easily modify using a word processor.

Web communities were perhaps the first new way that collaboration developed on the Internet. Most specialized fields have formed web communities where they share their latest insights and work. Web communities are also a powerful new way for learners to develop expertise. Brigid Barron (2006) describes how a high school girl found a website called Xanga (xanga.com) where digital artists talk about and share their work. She learned much by studying the source code that the artists used to produce the works she found most appealing. Web communities provide a new way to learn and share work.

Rebecca Black (2009) has been studying English language learners (ELLs) who participate in a fan fiction site (fanfiction.net) where they write their own stories taking off from books they love, such as the Harry Potter series. She focused her study on three girls: Grace from the Philippines, who began learning English in school at age 7; Nanako, who moved from Shanghai to Canada at 11; and Cherry-Chan, a Canadian who grew up speaking Mandarin and Taiwanese. To help learn English, the three girls wrote stories on the site, with help from readers on the site who would correct their spelling and grammar. Much of the feedback consisted of enthusiastic comments like "OMG! I love this!," which encouraged the girls to keep writing. Not only were they learning to read and write in English, but Black argues that their participation fostered their literacy development in three important ways: (1) It provided a sense of belonging in a community, (2) it provided confidence for attempting more complex endeavors, and (3) it enabled them to develop identities as creators and users of English. This is a powerful way to learn to read and write, as compared with what most ELL students endure.

As another example of how web communities help foster literacy, consider the Scratch community that Mitchel Resnick and his colleagues (2009) have developed. Scratch is a sophisticated computer-programming environment for children, used in schools and in computer clubhouses across the country. To complement the program, the Scratch developers have created a community bulletin board where Scratch users can show off their work and receive feedback and questions from other users, such as questions about how they created certain effects. One young girl developed a tutorial for other kids describing strategies for creating animé characters in Scratch, which she posted on the bulletin board. She received many comments applauding her for providing such a useful guide, as well as many suggestions for additions to her tutorial.

Video games use the narrative devices of roles and plots to draw players in with the immersive aspects of simulations. Many games exploit real-world situations and physical rules, but allow players to take on new roles and engage in adventures outside everyday experience. James Paul Gee (2003) describes how video games draw players into roles that may conflict with everyday values and encourage players to notice the gap with their own beliefs. In games like *Mass Effect* or *Command and Conquer*, for example, players take the roles of different sides in complex wars. To succeed in the game, players must understand the resources and capabilities of each side in the conflict, and then switch sides to take on the perspective of the enemy. Such role switching gives players the rare opportunity to see a conflict from multiple perspectives.

Video games are regarded as diversionary threats to the integrity of school (at best) or as destructive, compelling activities that simultaneously corrupt moral capacity and create a sedentary, motivation-destroying life-style. Just as schools are moving toward increasingly standardizing the learning experience, games offer the prospect of user-defined worlds in which players try out (and get feedback on) their own assumptions, strategies, and identities. Thus, games have come to typify the essentially subversive nature of computing in relation to schools.

Massively multiplayer online games (MMOGs) have led to an explosion of participation in virtual worlds, sometimes leading to addiction. Because many of these worlds are based on conflict and warfare, there is concern that playing them may foster aggressiveness among youth. Yet many players choose to develop trades and become merchants in games such as *Star Wars: Galaxies*. The vitality of these games depends upon players co-creating the world they inhabit. Students who may have little incentive to learn spelling and grammar for teachers in schools soon realize that the penalty for illiteracy in many online games is that players cannot communicate well with valued partners. In an online world, playing video games can take on new social and psychological dimensions. Gaming may help players learn a variety of skills, such as interviewing potential team members, negotiating with teammates and adversaries, assessing situations and risks, actively pursuing goals, and recovering from failures. As John Seely Brown and Douglas Thomas (2006) have suggested, the gamers of today may become the leaders of tomorrow.

Michele Knobel (2008), Kevin Leander and Gail Boldt (2008), and Don Leu (2010) have argued that teens are now using networked digital media for their ongoing business and social exchange. Teens are leading the way in using new digital media to blur the boundaries between personal communication, work, and learning. These authors argue that mastering digital media is giving rise to a new media literacy. This new literacy extends the decoding and manipulation skills of traditional print media by integrating video, images, music, and animation that give rise to new kinds of production. Teens are developing a sophisticated media literacy that is not taught in schools by creating webpages with animated computer graphics and sound, remixing images to develop music videos, participating in web chats and forums, and writing their own blogs.

To prepare students to communicate in this emerging world requires not simply traditional reading and writing, but also an understanding of how to communicate using different media with people who do not share the same assumptions. Sometimes this means reading multimedia documents that come from different sources. Other times, this means communicating with people via the Internet in different contexts, such as design projects, negotiation, and problem solving. Internet communication may involve texting, blogging, social network sites, chat rooms, video conferencing, and shared workspaces. Students need to learn to communicate in all these different contexts.

RETHINKING EDUCATION TO FOSTER LITERACY FOR ALL

Though the Internet has opened a variety of new ways for children to gain literacy skills, schools have been slow to incorporate these approaches into their teaching. As Rich Halverson and I (Collins & Halverson, 2009) have argued, there are deep incompatibilities between the culture of schooling and the imperatives of new technologies. For example, schools emphasize a core curriculum that every student must master, whereas technology allows kids to pursue their own interests and goals. Further, schools are expected to control what students do, whereas technology lets them explore the breadth of the web. Hence, K–12 schools have kept computers on the periphery, where they can control what students do when they are using them (Cuban, 2001). As a society, we need to think about how new technologies can be exploited in school for all children, whatever their background.

To help children acquire these new literacies, it behooves us as a society to ask questions like these:

- How can we give young children the tools to learn to read and write on their own?
- How can we create exciting games that require increasingly sophisticated literacy skills?
- How can we support children to find web communities that reflect their deep interests?
- How can we help children create a web identity that will appeal to other children in their community or the world?

Answers to these questions could profoundly affect literacy learning, but very few people are asking these questions. We need to radically rethink the ways to foster literacy development in the future.

One proposal is to give all young children in America a handheld device, stuffed with the best of children's literature, that can help them learn to read on their own (Collins & Halverson, 2009). There already are book apps that have many of these capabilities to support reading (Neary, 2011). Such a device could have easy-to-read stories like Dr. Seuss's *Green Eggs and Ham* enlivened with beautiful animation. Children would be able to point at difficult words or lines to hear them read aloud. Or they could opt to hear the entire story read aloud, with the words highlighted as they are read. There could be stories of interest to a wide spectrum of children, with support to help them find the kinds of stories they like best. And there could be games involving reading that children can play. It is important to research how best to entice children with different interests to teach themselves to read with such a device. But given very young children's fascination with smartphones and the Nintendo DS game system, it should not be difficult to produce handhelds that are potent environments for learning to read. It is critical to reach poor and minority children early with such devices, if they are going to develop strong literacy in English.

The Internet makes it possible for children to share what they read with children all over the world. It is important for students to read a lot, but educators should not be in the business of specifying particular books or stories that students should read. Some children may wish to read a lot of fiction and others may wish to read a lot of nonfiction. It would be good if students would write reviews and critiques of what they read, so that other students can find out what students think of different readings. Ideally, students should converse with like-minded students about things they both have read. The goal would be to set up interest groups on the web to help students find others who share their interests. Schools' responsibility in such a scheme is to ensure that students are reading and sharing what they learn, rather than testing them on their recall of what they read.

Idit Harel Caperton (www.worldwideworkshop.org) has been working with a variety of middle schools and high schools in West Virginia and Texas to develop digital literacies based on the Globaloria web platform. Participating students develop a game or simulation using the computer tools that Globaloria provides, working with support of older students, including some in college. The aim is to instill six learning abilities that are essential to success in college and the workplace:

1. The ability to invent, work through, and complete an original digital project for an educational web game or interactive simulation

2. The ability to manage a project online in a wiki-based networked environment
3. The ability to create digital media artifacts using wikis, blogs, and websites, and to publish and distribute these artifacts online
4. The ability for social-based learning, participation, and exchange across age groups and levels of expertise in a networked environment
5. The ability to use information as a learning tool, to search for information purposefully, and to explore information
6. The ability to surf websites and experiment with web applications and tools

These are the kinds of new literacies that will be required in the digital world our children are entering. And they are the kinds of literacies that few children acquire in school. The project is reaching a broad range of students that would not otherwise develop the new literacies required to succeed in the digital age.

The Digital Youth Network, a combined in-school and after-school program in Chicago, has worked to develop new literacy skills among middle school minority kids (Barron, Gomez, Pinkard, & Martin, 2014). This program offers both a wide array of special interest after-school clubs (such as robotics, graphic design, digital broadcast and moviemaking, music recording and remixing, and video game development) and mandatory media arts classes during the school day. The program provides artist-mentors to help guide the youths in developing their creations during after-school hours. It also developed a private social networking and learning online space called RemixWorld. In RemixWorld, students are able to share and critique videos, songs, podcasts, and graphic designs, and to dialogue through regular blog postings and discussion threads. The Digital Youth Network positions students as creative and critical producers. The artist-mentors help students look critically at ideas presented to them, and also create their own responses to what they see and hear. The students are learning to express their own ideas by producing original artifacts, and to respond to suggestions and critiques of their work.

These examples illustrate some of the ways schools can begin to address the equity issues raised by the advent of new media. Digital kids are growing used to controlling what they do with new media, and so it will become more and more difficult to teach literacy by giving them traditional reading and writing assignments. Now that the new technologies are empowering kids to pursue their own goals, they are becoming less willing to do whatever they are told, just like adults. We have to figure out ways to empower students to learn critical literacy skills while pursuing their own goals.

This is where the functionality of the skills we want them to learn becomes critical. Both Globaloria and the Digital Youth Network emphasize the idea of kids learning in what James Paul Gee (2003) refers to as "affinity spaces" and Henry Jenkins (2008) refers to as "participatory cultures." These social networks provide the glue that makes reading and writing and new forms of literacy meaningful to kids. To thrive in a digital world, students need to acquire these new literacy skills. As educators, our job is to make it possible for all kids to find a community where they are encouraged to be creative and constructive as they acquire new literacies.

WHAT PRACTICAL LITERACY SKILLS SHOULD STUDENTS LEARN?

For students to learn to communicate effectively in digital and other environments, there are some practical literacy skills that are critical: engaging in productive dialogue, persuading others about ideas, and negotiating effectively. Below, I address specific strategies that students need to learn in these three areas, which are rarely taught in schools.

Engaging in Productive Dialogue[2]

Dialogue has always taken place between individuals or groups of people gathered at the same time in the same place. But with the advent of computer technology, people are communicating with one another by texting and email; participating in chat rooms, forums, or web communities; and posting on blogs, Facebook, Twitter, and other social media sites. It almost seems as if many youths would rather interact over the Internet than talk face-to-face with the people they know (Turkle, 2015). Many of these new kinds of conversations are, in fact, learning conversations. As a society, we need to think about the implications of this transformation for education more generally.

These new forms of dialogue will inevitably change what and how students learn. Educators need to recognize these changes if they are going to design learning environments that are effective for the new generation of digital kids. We hear a lot about how easily young people are distracted by text messages and phone calls, causing some to argue that thinking is becoming shallower (Carr, 2011). We also hear about cyberbullying that the new media make so easy and anonymous—this is dialogue in its most dangerous form. On the positive side, the new media have led to more participation in dialogue by girls and shy people (Hsi & Hoadley, 1997).

---

2. This section is based on Collins and White (2015).

Sherry Turkle (2011), in her book *Alone Together*, worries that the increased dependence on texting is luring youth away from real conversation. Teens often say they prefer to text than to talk. She thinks they find that texting gives them more control, but at the sacrifice of depth and intimacy. They are sending out texts to multiple people instead of having one-on-one conversations with fewer people. School may become one of the last refuges for practicing and learning in-depth dialogue.

Productive dialogue does not come easily to people, especially to children who are engaging in more and more online dialogues with their peers. The research on "accountable talk" reveals how difficult it is for teachers to master the talk moves necessary to lead their students in conducting dialogues that are engaging and promote deep understanding (Michaels, O'Connor, & Resnick, 2008). Barbara White and John Frederiksen (2005) have developed an advisory system to teach young children working in groups to develop effective talk moves that lead them to probe more deeply into topics and to assess their own learning. The talk moves have been embedded in a computer system called the Web of Inquiry and, in simpler form, as printed guides to a set of roles, which 5th-grade students used to guide their inquiry when working in groups.

As students work together in groups to investigate research questions, each student plays a different managerial role, including cognitive roles (theory, evidence, synthesis, and application managers), social roles (collaboration, communication, mediation, and equity managers), and metacognitive roles (planning, productivity, reflection, and revision managers). In their groups, the 5th-graders started by playing the cognitive roles, went on to focus on the social roles, and finally played the metacognitive roles.

There is a one-page guide for each of these 12 roles. All the guides follow the same format. The four cognitive roles help students focus on understanding and working through their ideas. They push the group to articulate their ideas and cite evidence and applications for their ideas. Figure 2.1 illustrates the kinds of cognitive advice the children learn to use with the guide for the evidence manager.

The social advisors focused the group's efforts on sharing their work equitably, listening to one another, and working out their differences. Figure 2.2 illustrates what students learned about working together with the advice embedded in the communication manager.

The metacognitive advisors helped the students plan, monitor, revise, and reflect on their work. One of the metacognitive advisors, the planning manager, has basic advice about how to do planning. The guide for the planning manager is shown in Figure 2.3.

Figure 2.1. Evidence Manager

Goal 1: Find evidence and examples to support people's ideas.

Problem: There is no evidence to support an idea.
Strategy: Get people to produce good evidence for their ideas.
- What's your evidence for that?
- Can you give an example that supports your claim?

Strategy: Ask people to give reasons for their ideas.
- Why do you think that is true?
- Can you justify that idea?

Goal 2: Look for weaknesses in the support for an idea.

Problem: Some idea does not seem well supported.
Strategy: Get people to critique the evidence for each theory.
- I don't believe that because . . .
- Your evidence doesn't support your theory because . . .

Goal 3: Determine if people's arguments make sense.

Problem: The reasons for an idea aren't logical.
Strategy: Look for problems and holes in people's arguments.
- You didn't give a good argument for why you believe that . . .
- I am not convinced by your argument because . . .
- I think there's something missing in your argument . . .

Figure 2.2. Communication Manager

Goal 1: Listen to one another.

Problem: People aren't listening to one another.
Strategy: Find ways to get everyone to listen carefully and respectfully to what others say.
- Chris, can you explain what Sasha just said?
- Sasha made an important point. Did everyone get it?

Strategy: Get the group to treat everyone's ideas seriously.
- That's seems like an important idea . . .
- I like that idea because . . .

Goal 2: Build on one another's ideas.

Problem: People aren't benefiting from one another's input.
Strategy: Get people to connect what they say to what someone else said.
- What you just said makes me think about . . .
- Building on what Chris said, I think . . .

Goal 3: Develop a common, shared understanding.

Problem: People aren't understanding one another.
Strategy: Get the group to check on common understanding.
- Chris, did that make sense to you?
- I'm not sure what you mean. Can you explain it more?
- Do you mean . . .

Figure 2.3. Planning Manager

Goal 1: Decide on the goals.

Problem: The group can't figure out what it wants to do.
Strategy: Get the group to discuss what its goals should be.
- What are we trying to do?
- What are our priorities?

Goal 2: Develop a plan for achieving the goals.

Problem: We don't have a plan for how to accomplish our goals.
Strategy: Break the task into a sequence of steps.
- What should we do first?
- What's the next step?
- How should we do that step?

Goal 3: Figure out who will do what.

Problem: We can't agree on who should do what.
Strategy: Share the work fairly, considering everyone's interests and strengths.
- Should we do all the work together, or should we divide it up?
- Who wants to take charge of this task?

White and Frederiksen (2005; White, Frederiksen, & Collins, 2009) cite several kinds of evidence that children, when they play these roles for several months, begin to internalize the strategies, not just for their own roles, but also for the roles of others in their group. If children can learn to internalize the strategies and questions embedded in the guides, they should become better thinkers and be able to carry on better dialogues with one another. It is incredibly valuable to ask oneself the kinds of questions that the guides ask children to think about. Such knowledge could help learners working in environments, such as multiplayer games and Moose Crossing, to have more productive dialogues.

Carrying on productive dialogues is not easy. Though it is important for teachers to learn the talk moves that help children in their classrooms conduct productive dialogues, it is not enough. If children internalize the kinds of talk moves that the "accountable talk" research advocates (Michaels, O'Connor, & Resnick, 2008), they will be able to support dialogue, both in and out of classrooms, in order to pursue thinking more deeply. Dialogue is greatly expanding in digital environments where children are conversing with their peers. There is often no teacher to guide them in their learning. To make these conversations more productive, it is the educator's job to figure out how to teach children to internalize the talk moves that lead to productive dialogue. White and Frederiksen's work is a promising effort in that direction.

Being Persuasive

In many of the products students create and the interactions they have, both online and offline, they are trying to persuade others to do or believe something that will help the students realize their goals. It is critical that schools teach the knowledge and skills students need to be convincing.

The strategies for being persuasive are much the same in speaking, writing, and interacting in digital media. But each medium has its own special properties. Face-to-face conversations are helpful in negotiating complex issues where misunderstandings can occur and need to be detected and resolved in order to reach an understanding. Written communications are effective for communicating complex ideas where people may need to go back over the text and figures to understand the meaning. Videos are very compelling and give viewers a sense of involvement. Understanding the power and limitations of different media is becoming critical to persuasion in today's world (Collins, Neville, & Bielaczyc, 2000; Poe, 2011).

Students need to be taught the critical elements that make an argument substantive, convincing, interesting, understandable, and memorable (Collins & Gentner, 1980). There are various strategies for achieving each of these objectives.

- *Substantive.* A substantive argument makes important points that address issues people care about. It contains novel ideas and arguments that make people think about things in a new way. It focuses on ideas that are central to the argument and not extraneous to the points being made. In short, it contains content that is both useful and important.
- *Convincing.* A convincing argument is important, logical, and well grounded. In writing, this requires justification at many different levels as to why the reader should care. Students need to provide evidence, such as data and sources, to back up their claims, and the logic of the argument needs to be made very clear. In conversation, students should try to find out where their listeners are coming from and address the issues they are concerned about. In framing any argument, students need to think about how the audience views the world and build upon this view by emphasizing why it matters to the audience.
- *Interesting.* Two aspects can make an argument interesting. First, students must entice listeners or readers to pay attention and then must hold their interest. In order to get their attention, students need to begin with novel insights or stories that illustrate the issues,

just as newspaper and magazine articles do. Foreshadowing what is to come, as suspense does in fiction, can increase the reader's or listener's interest in staying with the argument, as do stories, humor, and metaphors throughout.

- **Understandable.** Students need to figure out the interests, needs, and abilities of the audience and use terms that will be familiar. Children require much simpler arguments than adults. But it is always a good strategy to explain an idea the audience may not have encountered before. Professional writers use short paragraphs and sentences, because these enable readers to stop frequently to make sure they understand. It is critical to be coherent, avoiding side trips into extraneous issues. And providing an overall structure, with a preview of where the text is going and a recapitulation at the end, helps readers or listeners follow the argument and know what to take away.

- **Memorable.** Provocative stories and metaphors, which make an argument interesting, can also help make it stick in the mind. But among other strategies for making an argument memorable, perhaps the most important is providing a meme or short phrase that captures the essence of the argument and can easily be stored in memory. It also helps to include graphics, such as tables, graphs, diagrams, pictures, or animations, that represent the essential elements of the ideas involved. Too many graphic representations, however, can obscure the key ideas. People remember stories and visuals better than they remember logic and arguments, so stories and graphics can help ensure memorability.

Persuasion is central to leadership and living a successful life. In her Design Club, Marcela Borge (Borge, Yan, Shimoda, & Toprani, in press; Jung & Borge, 2016) has middle school students working with other students to develop designs for constructions of their own choosing, such as a haunted house. Working in groups, they first make pencil-and-paper drawings of their designs. Then they create LEGO models of their designs, and finally they work online in Minecraft to create an online version of their design. In developing their designs, kids have to negotiate what they will design, who will do what, and how to integrate all their ideas into a coherent design. Borge and her colleagues help the kids develop norms for working together and resolving their differences. She also has kids who develop ideas that are useful for the entire class make presentations to the class as a whole. In their negotiations and presentations, kids are learning how to persuade others to adopt their ideas and work to implement them. Persuasion is a critical skill whenever people need to communicate and work together.

Negotiating Effectively

Almost all interactions in work and family situations require negotiation. In school, negotiation arises whenever students work together on projects. When a school emphasizes groupwork, it is preparing students for the kind of situations that are becoming more prevalent in a world where individuals are interacting with many others coming from different backgrounds and cultures.

Roger Fisher, William Ury, and Bruce Patton (1991), in their book *Getting to Yes*, describe an approach to negotiating that is much more effective than arguing from opposing positions, which characterizes most negotiations. They suggest an approach involving four strategies. I will briefly describe their arguments for each of these strategies and relate them to student negotiators:

1. *Separate the people from the problem.* In most negotiations, it is important to maintain a good relationship with the other side. Often the relationship gets entangled with the problem, so that if one says, "This plan is a mess," it is likely to be taken as criticism of others rather than as an objective statement that there is a problem to be solved. If one interprets what someone else says as criticism, emotions tend to escalate and undermine the trust needed for successful negotiation. It helps to make conciliatory gestures when emotions have exploded, such as reassuring the other person. It is not helpful to make accusations such as "You said you would." The goal should be to develop a relationship where students are working together to solve a problem, rather than treating one another as adversaries. In her Design Club, Borge and her colleagues get the kids to develop norms of politeness in order to facilitate negotiations.

2. *Focus on interests rather than on positions.* Suppose two students are asked to design a computer program to teach fractions to young children. One wants to have players divide up cookies to serve different numbers of kids fairly. The other wants to design a game where players have to guess where the sum of two fractions will fall on a number line from 0 to 2. The teacher might suggest how the students can include both ideas in their program, by dividing up cookies fairly and having the user guess where the fraction falls on a number line. As Fisher et al. (1991) point out, the basic problem in negotiation "lies not in conflicting positions, but in the conflict between each side's needs, desires, concerns, and fears" (p. 40). In order to find the best solution to a problem, it is

these interests one needs to address. By looking behind opposing positions, one can often find an alternative that satisfies the interests of both sides.

3. ***Invent options for mutual gain.*** As Fisher et al. (1991) point out, one skilled negotiator they know attributes his success to inventing "solutions advantageous to both his client and the other side" (p. 56). In many negotiations, the only creative thinking involved is to split the difference. To create more options, Fisher et al. recommend setting up a *brainstorming* session where the focus is on coming up with possible solutions to the problem. The critical strategy in brainstorming is to generate options without critiquing them. It is helpful to work together around a whiteboard to come up with possible options, guided by a facilitator. After brainstorming, the goal is to pick out the most promising ideas, invent ways to improve these ideas, and then set up a way to decide which of the options to advance in negotiation.

4. ***Resolve differences by using objective criteria.*** Finding objective criteria can lead to an amicable resolution of differences. How might one establish objective criteria? For example, in designing a program to teach fractions as described above, the designers could put together a questionnaire to test out which ideas for activities appeal most to young children, and have a teacher give the questionnaire to a class of children who are learning about fractions. The children could rate the ideas on a five-point scale as to how interesting they would find the different activities.

Currently, most schools do not teach students negotiation skills, and yet these skills are becoming more important as routine work disappears and workplaces require people to work together to accomplish corporate goals. With divorce increasing, negotiating skills are also needed in the home to keep couples together. The social roles described earlier that White and Frederiksen (1998) developed help students practice negotiation skills. Schools would do well to teach negotiation to students to prepare them for the adult world they are entering.

TEACHING THE NEW LITERACY TO ALL STUDENTS

In *Rethinking Education in the Age of Technology*, Richard Halverson and I (Collins & Halverson, 2009) argued that much of education is moving out of the schools and into other venues where learners are free to pursue their own interests and goals. Schools need to find ways to harness these new technologies not just for the elites whose children are using technology in innovative ways, but for all children, whatever their background.

This requires educators to incorporate creative uses of technology into literacy education, such as those found in fan fiction sites, multiplayer games, the Scratch community, Globaloria, and the Digital Youth Network. Students need to be engaged in creating their own products that they publish for others to see, interpret, and critique. They need guidance from mentor teachers and others on to how to improve their work and how to reach an audience. This requires a radical rethinking of how we teach literacy, in order to prepare students for the kinds of challenges they face in the digital world.

CHAPTER 3

Developing Self-Sufficiency

In her book *Mindset*, Carol Dweck (2008) quotes a 7th-grade girl: "I think intelligence is something you have to work for . . . it isn't just given to you. . . . Most kids, if they're not sure of an answer, will not raise their hand to answer the question. But what I usually do is raise my hand, because if I'm wrong, then my mistake will be corrected. Or I will raise my hand and say 'How would this be solved?' or 'I don't get this. Can you help me?' Just by doing that I'm increasing my intelligence" (p. 17).

Dweck focuses her book around the difference between people who have a fixed-intelligence mindset versus a growth mindset. She finds that a lot of people, both young and old, believe that intelligence is fixed at birth and that what they need to do to get through life is look good and not make any mistakes. Hence, they avoid challenges, so they won't fail. Others, like the 7th-grader quoted above, have a growth mindset. They love challenges and they want to get smarter. As Benjamin Barber, an eminent sociologist, once said: "I don't divide the world into the weak and the strong, or the successes and the failures. . . . I divide the world into the learners and the nonlearners" (quoted in Dweck, 2008, p. 16).

Having a strategic mindset is critical to navigating through today's complex world. There are a lot of techniques individuals can employ when they want to be strategic, as our 7th-grade girl suggests. There are strategies for asking questions and collecting information. And there are strategies for planning what they will do, monitoring their progress, and reflecting on what they could have done better. In this chapter, I enumerate some of the strategies that are worth having students learn as well as the dispositions that are critical for employing the strategies most effectively.

Planning, monitoring, and reflection are the basic elements of the learning cycle that pervades everything we do. When we do something that is at all complicated, success often depends on how well we plan to approach the task and how well we monitor our progress in carrying it out. Reflection is critical to doing similar tasks better in the future, so when we plan our next activity we need to look back at what we have learned from similar things we have done. Most people do too little planning, monitoring, and reflecting, and so they do not learn much from the things they do. To be strategic, individuals need to be much more aware of what they are doing and what they can learn from what they do.

I used to tell my students, "I worked at the same research firm for 30 years, but none of you ever will, given the way the world is changing." Firms are being bought up these days, leading to frequent reorganizations and layoffs. New technologies are disrupting the old ways of doing things, destroying businesses such as newspapers and bookstores. Freelancing is taking hold in many industries like taxi service and college teaching, driving down costs and eliminating benefits for workers. These disruptions put everyone at risk of facing sudden changes in their lives.

As society evolves toward more independent living and working in what is called the "gig economy," people must become more self-sufficient. These societal changes are producing an "Uber generation," where people are often working as independent operators who manage their own lives. It harkens back to an agricultural society where families operated independently, often at the mercy of the economy, the weather, and disease. This new economy requires that folks understand complex issues of health, finance, and law in order to make wise personal decisions. Furthermore, people must learn to exercise self-control over their lives and decisions. There is abundant evidence that self-regulatory skills are central to living a happy and successful life. Recent studies have shown that it is possible to learn these skills, but they are seldom taught in school, except in extracurricular activities. They need to become central to the school curriculum.

THE GROWING NEED FOR SELF-RELIANCE

In agricultural societies that predated industrialization, people lived insecure lives. There were many threats to their well-being. Fire might burn down their house or their farm buildings. Disease or accidents might cripple their ability to work. Storms or pests might damage their crops. Financial panics might wipe out their assets. Life was precarious. The lucky thrived and some became rich, while the majority survived as best they could.

In the 20th century, the developed world figured out how to ameliorate these risks and provide more security for the average person. People found jobs in towns and cities, which developed fire departments that protected people and their property. Doctors, hospitals, and public health agencies became much more capable of treating and preventing illness and healing injuries from accidents. Governments became more savvy at preventing financial panics. And many governments developed social safety nets to protect people when they were laid off work or retired, and to provide help when illness or disasters strike. People in the developed world have become used to feeling more secure against life's vicissitudes.

But what technology gave us, it is now beginning to take away. One of the first inklings of what we now see occurring widely happened in the movie industry in the late 20th century. It used to be that actors were employed by movie studios, which paid their salaries and decided what movies to make and who should direct and act in them. The studios did all the hiring and firing, all the distribution and publicity. They took care of everything. But the studio system slowly fell apart as actors and directors took more power onto themselves. They put projects together, hiring people they liked to work with and selling their completed projects to studios, which still handled the distribution and publicity.

For example, at a party, well-known actor Ethan Hawke met a former concert pianist named Seymour Bernstein. Bernstein, then in his late 80s, had abandoned his career at age 50 because of stage fright. He had retreated to a modest career as a teacher and composer. Hawke told his wife that somebody ought to make a movie about Bernstein, and she suggested that he should be the one to do it. Hawke put together a team of people to make the movie *Seymour: An Introduction*, which shows Bernstein's love of music and teaching to great critical acclaim. It is a movie that would never have been made under the old studio system.

This kind of freelancing is now spreading to every aspect of society, driven by computer networks. People are hiring other individuals on a short-term basis as drivers and to do household chores, run errands, and provide overnight accommodations. Companies nowadays prefer to hire freelancers to work on a particular project, and those freelancers go on to other things when the project ends. The freelancing life is more precarious than a secure job with benefits. Freelancers have to please their customers and hustle to keep employed. They have to be much more self-reliant. It is not an easy life. People have to be strategic to thrive as part of the Uber generation.

The trend toward freelancing puts new demands on what students need to learn to be successful. Students must learn to be self-sufficient, which means understanding how to manage their health and finances. They must understand the law and the rights and responsibilities it entails. They must learn to be strategic and control their impulses. They must learn how to please clients and build trusting relationships with them.

WHAT SHOULD STUDENTS LEARN
ABOUT MAINTAINING A HEALTHY LIFESTYLE?

In a freelance economy, people need to take care of their health so that they can remain productive, because they will not have paid sick days. In their book *Younger Next Year*, Chris Crowley and Dr. Henry S. Lodge (2004) write:

> Some 70 percent of premature death and aging is lifestyle-related. Heart attacks, strokes, the common cancers, diabetes, most falls, fractures, and serious injuries, and many more illnesses are primarily caused by the way we live. If we had the will to do it, we could eliminate more than half of all disease in men and women over fifty. Not delay it, eliminate it. That is a readily obtainable goal, but we are not moving toward it. Instead, we have made these problems invisible by making them part of the "normal" landscape of aging. (p. 29)

Crowley and Lodge argue that if we adopt a lifestyle involving daily exercise, good nutrition, emotional commitment, and "real engagement with living," we can all live much healthier lives until our 80s or 90s. This is not simply a recipe for old people. It is a recipe for children, for young adults, for the middle-aged, as well as for the old. Much of the damage we do to our bodies starts early in life with high stress, poor diet, risky behavior, and lack of exercise. When we are young, we often don't feel the effects of the way we mistreat our bodies—but those effects show up later in life. And most people don't realize the problems they are causing themselves in the future. Students should learn how to take much better care of themselves if they want to live a healthy life as adults.

It does not make sense that people know so little about how to preserve their health. This is a matter of life and death, and yet ignorance is rampant. Although schools teach the sciences of biology, chemistry, geology, and physics, which have little real impact on people's lives, the curriculum largely ignores health. Students may take a single health class, but health is not deeply embedded in the school curriculum. Yet health is a science that really matters for people's lives.

The three major strategies for reducing health problems are lowering stress, actively exercising almost every day, and eating a nutritious diet. Students need to learn prevention strategies in order to live a healthy life and thrive in their future careers.

Teaching Students to Lower Their Stress

High stress is one of the major causes of both physical and mental health problems. Many kinds of events can cause stress in people, such as a tornado or flood, or a rare life event such as losing a job. But much more commonly, stress results from daily events like working with difficult people, dealing with financial problems, or facing frequent deadlines. These daily events cause chronic stress that over time can lead to a variety of health problems, including high blood pressure, heart arrhythmia, heart disease, stroke, cancer, arthritis, fatigue, anxiety, depression, infertility, asthma, and immune system suppression (Graham, Christian, & Kiecolt-Glaser, 2006). Students should investigate the effects of stress and how they can learn to cope with the stresses in their own lives.

Much of the stress in students' lives comes from social pressures and deadlines in schools. Social pressures have been heightened in the digital world by the need for "likes" on Facebook and the growth of anonymous bullying. Students need guidance in learning to deal with stressors at this stage and how to apply such strategies in their future lives.

Drs. Stephen Sinatra and James Roberts (2007), in their book *Reverse Heart Disease Now*, outline a variety of strategies that adults can use to reduce stress, and these techniques can be adapted for young people. Combating stress often requires dramatic changes in lifestyle. The first point Sinatra and Roberts emphasize is that stress is not what happens to individuals, but how people react to what happens. Interpreting things calmly and rationally rather than panicking emotionally is the first step to a cure for chronic stress. In his high school health class, a teacher in San Francisco teaches three strategies to reduce stress: deep breathing, visualization of a relaxing place, and progressive relaxation (Pepper, 2012).

Sinatra and Roberts (2007) also recommend meditation to reduce stress. The practice of meditation has been shown to effectively reduce stress, lower blood pressure, and increase life expectancy. Meditation is a part of yoga programs that emphasize exercise and deep breathing. In 2007, one middle school in a high-crime area of San Francisco introduced a 12-minute period of meditation at the start and end of the school day (Pepper, 2012). The students were living very stressful lives, with many homicides occurring in their neighborhood. The intervention reduced the truancy rate and the suspension rate for students in the school by half. In schools where meditation has been introduced, students show positive effects such as less stress, improved academic achievement, better focus, reduced depression and anxiety, reduced addiction, and better behavior (tmhome.com/benefits/10-benefits-of-meditation-for-students/).

Sinatra and Roberts (2007) cite the American Heart Association, which makes a number of recommendations for reducing stress:

- Talk to trusted friends and advisors about your stresses and ask for their support.

- Learn to accept things you can't change.
- Count to ten before responding when you are angry.
- Don't use smoking, drinking, overeating, drugs, or caffeine to cope with stress. They make things worse.
- Look for the good in situations instead of the bad.
- Exercise regularly, doing something you enjoy.
- Be an animal caregiver, since people with pets see doctors less often and have lower blood pressure.
- Think ahead to what may upset you and avoid it, such as people who bother you.
- Plan productive solutions to problems and set clear limits on what you do for family.
- Learn to say no. Don't promise too much and give yourself enough time to get things done.
- Join a support group for the kind of people you identify with. (pp. 197–198)

Students can investigate how these strategies help reduce stress and develop action plans for implementing the strategies in their lives. They also need to study how stress affects the body and engage in projects that identify the triggers for stress. Wellness should be a central focus of study beginning in the first years of school. Teachers need to develop a collaborative culture that respects different students' contributions and in which students work together in groups to meet deadlines. In this kind of project culture, teachers can coach students to develop work habits and practices that reduce stress, such as meditation.

Encouraging Students to Exercise Regularly

In a world of video games and reduced physical activities at school in favor of test preparation, students are getting less and less exercise. This is a recipe for declining health and obesity. As Crowley and Lodge argue, humans evolved in a world where they often had to run for their lives, avoiding predators and chasing game to find enough food to eat. In developed countries, we can avoid predators and get enough food, though we hardly move a muscle. Crowley and Lodge suggest, "This is arguably the most profound shift, ever, in the way the world works. . . . Our minds do not know how to 'read' the absence of danger, the absence of the need to hunt and gather— the idleness. And we soften to death. . . . Our lifestyle is a disease more deadly than cancer, war, or plague. We live longer because of modern medicine, but many of us live wretchedly and many of us die much younger than we should" (p. 46). Much of this modern problem comes from sitting for long periods of time, instead of moving around the grasslands and forests. If people want to live a long and healthy life, they have to keep moving. They need to learn about the importance of regular exercise.

To stay healthy, the body must keep replacing old cells with new ones, because old cells tend to get cancer. Exercise helps tear down old cells and build new ones. It releases hormones that cause inflammation to attack dying cells and other hormones to help build new cells. Chronic stress causes the inflammation that kills cells without providing the hormones that build new cells. In adults, things like commuting, deadlines, financial problems, loneliness, and too much alcohol all trigger inflammation, but not renewal. As Crowley and Lodge argue, exercise is the foundation for positive brain chemistry; a healthy immune system; better sleep; weight loss and insulin regulation; and resistance to heart attack, stroke, cancer, Alzheimer's disease, arthritis, diabetes, and depression. Exercise is a "wonder drug," a kind of magic elixir.

Heart disease is the leading cause of death in the developed world. The large majority of adults have heart disease although many don't know it. Crowley and Lodge claim, "Vigorous exercise, the real thing, cuts your risk of dying of a heart attack by half" (p. 75). Cholesterol from all the cheese, butter, sugar, red meat, and French fries that young people eat causes blockages in their arteries. As a blockage builds up, it can break loose and get carried to the small arteries that lead to the heart or brain—which is the mechanism of a heart attack or stroke. Exercise counters this scenario by building new blood vessels and repairing damage to old ones. To prevent heart disease, students need to change their diets and exercise more.

Alzheimer's disease affects more and more people as we live longer—some researchers think it affects half of people over 85 ("Dementia," 2015). The epidemic of Alzheimer's is pushing up the cost of health care enormously. Students need to learn that physical exercise is the most effective means to prevent and treat Alzheimer's. Studies in humans show that exercise leads to decreased amounts of plaque in the brain, and a study showed that mice that exercised had 50% to 80% less plaque in their brains than mice whose exercise was restricted (Lippert, 2009). There are also indications that people who have more education and are active mentally, learning new things, are less likely to get Alzheimer's. Any measures students learn about to prevent Alzheimer's are extremely worthwhile.

Aerobic exercise is critical to most of the health benefits that exercise provides. Students can get aerobic exercise by vigorous walking, running, swimming, biking, skating, jumping rope, and regularly playing any number of sports, such as basketball or tennis. They should be encouraged to choose an activity they enjoy, or else they won't keep it up regularly. Crowley and

Lodge argue that the "sweet spot" with exercise comes from about 45 minutes each day. They recommend 4 or 5 days of aerobic exercise and 2 or 3 days of strength and balance exercises.

Public health officials recommend that schools provide an hour of exercise every day, but most states do not require schools to do so, and schools have been cutting back on exercise programs in an effort to improve test scores (Park, 2016). Research shows that engaging students in active exercise at school does not decrease test scores and sometimes improves them (Basch, 2011). Schools need to engage all students, particularly girls and minorities, each day in an active exercise program for at least 45 minutes. It will improve their health and help them see the positive effects of exercise.

Teaching Students to Eat a Nutritious Diet

Obesity has become a major problem in America because many young people and families are not eating a healthy diet. Obesity is leading to an epidemic of diabetes and heart disease that may well shorten American life expectancy. Combating obesity is a major issue, because obesity drives up health care costs that are already out of control. It is a growing problem as we eat more fast food, spend more screen time, and get less exercise (National Heart, Lung, and Blood Institute, 2012). Former First Lady Michelle Obama led an effort to get schools to address the problem of childhood obesity and take measures to reverse the trends that have taken root in America, leading to poor health (www.letsmove.gov/about).

What students need to know about a healthy diet can be stated fairly simply (Pollan, 2009): Eat a lot of vegetables, fruits, nuts, and foods rich in fiber. Don't eat a lot of refined starches, sugary food and drinks, saturated fats, salt, red meat, and processed foods. Of course, much of the food industry is trying to sell people foods that are bad for their health. Worse yet, most people would agree that many unhealthy foods, such as doughnuts, cheeseburgers, French fries, ice cream, and soda, taste delicious. The makers of these products have figured out how to exploit their advantage, and they will not surrender it easily.

Health science should be a central theme of education in schools. For example, students might carry out investigations about how exercise affects various systems in the body, how carbohydrates affect weight, and why dietary guidelines have changed over the years. They also might address other critical health issues that students face such as pregnancy, suicide prevention, and addiction (including gambling, video games, drugs, and alcohol). Focusing students on investigating health issues will help them be much more involved in making sense of how stress, exercise, and diet affect their health. Such investigations will have a much greater impact than would be the case if students are simply fed guidelines on what steps to take to ensure good health, as traditional health classes have done.

WHAT SHOULD STUDENTS LEARN
ABOUT FINANCIAL AND LEGAL MATTERS?

In a gig economy, people need to understand the financial and legal matters they will face as freelancers interacting with the clients they need to cultivate to earn a living. As problems arise, they will have to make key financial decisions, such as what health insurance to buy, how can they save and invest money for retirement, and how to deal with clients who fail to pay their bills. Students will need to develop skills to deal with such problems in order to develop self-reliance. Making wise financial and legal decisions is critical to survival as a freelancer.

Finance

The first thing students should learn is to cultivate the habit of seeking out financial information from diverse sources. This can involve listening to financial news on TV and radio, reading financial publications, and talking to knowledgeable friends. Developing financial wisdom takes work.

Financial wisdom also requires planning. Students need to learn how to investigate questions such as: Is it better to invest in stocks, bonds, or real estate to provide income for the future? What kinds of insurance are necessary and best to purchase in different circumstances? How much money does one need in reserve against possible setbacks, like the loss of a job? Most people do not like to do much planning, preferring to be more spontaneous. That may work for day-to-day living, but planning is essential when it comes to finances.

Students should learn how to deal with setbacks in their financial situation. Elizabeth Warren and Amelia Warren Tyagi (2003) have studied what causes middle-class Americans to go into bankruptcy. They found that bankruptcy is usually caused by the loss of a job or large medical expenses. Americans have been living too close to the edge with few savings to fall back on. Sometimes they buy a home that is too costly for them because it is in a neighborhood with good schools for their children. Sometimes they buy expensive cars that they have to pay off over time. The amount of personal debt in the United States reached a historic high before the recession of 2008, and the savings rate had fallen to zero or below. This was unsustainable. Since the recession, Americans have started saving again, but at a lower rate than they did before the invention of credit cards.

There is no problem with credit cards if people pay off their balance each month, but the industry figured out how to lure people into accumulating more debt by encouraging them to pay a low monthly fee, which hardly reduced the amount they owed. People who were short of money took this fee as the amount they should pay each month. At the same time, the industry charged very high interest rates on the balance after their low-cost teaser rates expired. Interest rates on most credit card debt and payday loans today would have been considered usury in an earlier era. People would do well to confine their debt to fixed-rate mortgages and car loans.

Economists have a basic principle about "sunk costs." In common parlance, this goes by the phrase, "Don't pour good money after bad." The principle applies not just to money, but to any other cost, such as time and effort. The principle says that as you proceed in any effort, you should weigh at each moment in time whether the expected future payoff is greater than the expected future cost. If the expected costs outweigh the benefits, you should abandon the endeavor. This is very difficult for people to do when they have invested money or effort into something. There are psychic costs that go along with abandoning any effort, and in some cases, there are also real social costs. Nevertheless, the principle should be followed as best as possible, given that people waste an enormous amount of money and effort pursuing unlikely endeavors.

There are many programs that teach financial literacy to students (www.edutopia.org/financial-literacy-resources-guide). Some elementary schools work with a local bank or credit union to come into school once a week for kids to deposit money into a savings account. The students learn about saving for long-term goals, deposit slips, interest, and how money accumulates over time. Students learn to plan and think about saving goals, like the money they will need for college. In one middle school program, the computer science, art, and technology teachers, with the help of a local candy company, got the kids to create their own candy company in just 2 weeks. This meant learning how to design a chocolate bar, creating the mold for it, pouring the chocolate, designing a company logo, creating a business plan, creating company business cards, and finally creating a 30-second video ad marketing the chocolate bar.

A high school project helped students think about what it takes to buy a home. They helped a graduate from their school build his first home with Habitat for Humanity and heard how he put together the financing. Then they studied the trade-offs between renting and buying and what it takes to be able to buy, including a good credit score and a down payment. They projected their earnings in a career they hoped to pursue and talked to bank credit officers about financing a house on their projected earnings.

Another school had upperclassmen prepare short videos on their plans to pay for college, which the students evaluated together for the feasibility and quality of the presentation. Engaging students in dealing with real-world financial problems helps them relate what they learn to the problems they will face when they go out into the world.

Making wise financial and economic decisions is very difficult and important for success in life. It is not something people can offload to a financial advisor. Such advisors can be helpful, but to be successful people need to take responsibility for their own financial decisionmaking. Students can learn about financial matters by budgeting and keeping track of costs and earnings from the school projects they engage in. It is critical that all our citizens understand economics and finance. But there is little attention paid to these topics in our schools, and it clearly shows in the level of public discourse on economic matters. It is important for our students to become much smarter about finance and economics.

Law

To manage life in a gig economy, students need to learn about their legal rights and responsibilities. The legal system is complicated, and students need to know when to seek legal counsel. It is critical for students to understand some of the basic legal situations that may arise in everyday life, such as contracts, torts, arrests, divorce, and bullying. In this section, I discuss some ways in which students can learn about the legal system.

We all make contracts when we buy a home, join Facebook, hire a plumber, or visit the doctor. Some contracts are written, such as a mortgage or a Facebook agreement; others may be oral, as with the plumber; and some may be implicit, as with the doctor. Contracts involve a promise of some exchange, such as a service performed or an item delivered in exchange for money. There also is an assumption that the exchange is legally binding, though that may be voided for minors or the mentally ill. Most people do not read written contracts, such as with Facebook, but they are still bound legally if they sign up.

If students become freelancers, they are likely to encounter cases of tort law. Torts are cases where a person sues for damages they have suffered from some transaction. In one famous tort case, a woman in Texas sued McDonald's restaurants when she suffered severe burns from spilling McDonald's coffee on herself (en.wikipedia.org/wiki/McDonald%27s_coffee_case). Her claim was that the coffee was much hotter than coffee served at other restaurants, and was inherently dangerous. A jury awarded her $2.86 million, including punitive damages, though the judge reduced the award to $640,000. The case was finally settled out of court when McDonald's appealed the decision. Students might investigate various kinds of tort cases to see what factors determine their outcomes, as well as engaging in mock trials to decide difficult cases involving the kinds of issues students are likely to face in their lives. (Teachers can find sample trials at teachingcivics.org/lesson/mini-mock-trials.).

Students should also learn about criminal law. Mock cases and trials are an excellent way to teach students about the criminal justice system. One case that has been developed for schools involves a 19-year-old driver making a turn and hitting a young cyclist who rode illegally on a downtown sidewalk and darted suddenly into the crosswalk (teachingcivics.org/wordpress/wp-content/uploads/2013/06/State-v.-Max-Paulson-Mock-Trial.pdf). The driver did not see the cyclist coming, but was charged with reckless driving. The cyclist suffered a broken leg in the accident. This type of case brings to life the kinds of legal problems students are likely to face, and forces them to work through the steps of the legal process in a difficult case.

With the increase in divorce rates, students should also learn the basics of divorce law in America. The legal battles in most divorces are fought over alimony or legal rights with regard to children. Custody of children is frequently awarded to mothers, with visitation rights to fathers. In recent times, awarding joint custody to both parents has become more common, especially when the divorce is amicable. Students should investigate how different states handle divorce and analyze the pros and cons of different approaches.

Bullying has become more of a problem in recent years because of social media that can expose verbal and physical abuse to a much larger audience. Sometimes this involves spreading sexually explicit materials over the Internet, which can have devastating social consequences for a person. In her book *Sticks and Stones*, Emily Bazelon (2013) warns about criminalizing children's bullying, because of the risk of harming young people who make mistakes. At the same time, she argues that society should work to create a culture where bullying is strongly discouraged. The pervasive use of social media has made bullying a major problem among today's youth. It would be good to involve older students in helping to settle cases of school bullying where they do not know the parties involved and can act impartially.

Students need to learn about the basics of the law that they are likely to encounter. Older students need to investigate issues of institutional racism and arrest practices that are central to much of the controversy stirring modern economies, particularly those with issues of racial integration and immigration. By investigating issues of fairness and justice in different contexts, students will come to appreciate the procedures and nuances of the law as it applies in their society, and ideally will become informed citizens with an interest in improving legal procedures.

WHAT SHOULD STUDENTS LEARN ABOUT STRATEGY AND SELF-REGULATION?

To survive in a gig economy, students need to learn to be strategic in navigating through a complex world. This involves dealing with other people, regulating their own impulses, planning and monitoring their actions, reflecting on what they could do better, and adapting to the situations in which they find themselves. To learn these strategic skills, they need to work on projects that require them to think strategically and adapt to new challenges and opportunities. This kind of psychological knowledge, called "executive function," can pay huge dividends in adult life (Mischel, 2014).

Being Strategic in Relating to Others

In navigating through the social world, it is necessary to be strategic in dealing with other people who have competing objectives. Unfortunately, schools don't teach much about how to be strategic in negotiating with the world. And as the world gets more complex, it gets harder to figure out what to do in different situations. I will identify a few critical strategies.

A compelling story about a failure to negotiate involves two leading American scientists during the 1800s who were both fossil hunters (www. pbs.org/wgbh/americanexperience/features/biography/dinosaur-rivalry/). One of them, O. C. Marsh, was a professor at Yale, and the other, Edward Cope, was affiliated with the Philadelphia Museum of Natural History. Marsh wanted to control the collection of fossils in America. Cope felt his trust was violated after he showed Marsh a rich fossil site, whereupon Marsh made arrangements for all the fossils from the site to be sent to Marsh himself. Later, when both men sought out dinosaur bones across the West, they engaged in a fierce competition. They ended up destroying each other, and both lost many of their prized fossils in later life. The two would have done much better to negotiate a way of searching for fossils without stepping on each other. After all, it is a big country with a lot of fossils.

The ability to see what is really going on around you is called "situational awareness." This is a disposition that everyone needs to cultivate. Students need to pay attention to the intentions and goals of all the people they are dealing with. This may require asking other people what they are trying to accomplish and reading between the lines of their answers. Often, people may not quite know the game others are playing, or why they are doing what they are doing. If a person gets angry or does something that harms someone else, it is strategic not to interpret their actions personally. It may be that the person is just in a bad mood or does not realize that their actions have such a negative effect. Negotiating with people about the problem is a much better strategy than retaliating, as both Cope and Marsh tried to do. Of course, negotiation may not have worked, but it is always worth a try.

Dealing with people who have power or represent a threat in some way is obviously a tricky business. But it is crucial to teach students the skills to do this. For example, it is strategic to help powerful people achieve their goals, to the degree it does not undermine one's own values and goals. If your own values are undermined in some way, it is best to walk away. Whistleblowing is worthwhile, but only when one is safely out from under the power of the adversary. Cope was able to bring down Marsh, who schemed against him, once Cope had given up his fossil hunting.

When engaged in such a struggle, it is critical not to act impulsively or emotionally. Students need to learn to calculate the best strategy for dealing with the situation. Forming alliances with others who are in the same situation is often the most effective strategy for dealing with someone who is more powerful. But above all, an individual must preserve his or her reputation as fair and reasonable.

Evidence has been piling up in recent years that we developed our big brains in order to interact with other people. School hardly teaches how to do that at all. And so most people have to learn such tricks on their own. As described in Chapter 2, Barbara White and John Frederiksen (2005) taught productive strategies for working with other students by having students take on different roles as they worked on projects together. Similarly, Marcela Borge and her colleagues (in press) teach many of the strategies needed to get along with others in their Design Club, where they get students to develop norms of behavior for interacting with others. Students will be more successful in life if they are taught or can find a mentor to help them learn strategies for relating to others.

Improving Students' Self-Control

Teaching students to develop the skills of self-regulation is critical for living and working with others. Students should investigate the long-term benefits of self-control and practice strategies for self-control as they work on projects in school. Psychologists Ed Diener and his son Robert (Diener & Biswas-Diener, 2008) argue that regulating negative emotions is an important aspect of self-control: "For some people, anger is exciting, and they can learn to feed off the negative emotional dramas in their lives. For other people, self-pity can act as a blanket, one that individuals can swaddle themselves in for a kind of perverse security" (p. 23).

Leading psychologist Martin Seligman (1994) describes how anger can destroy people's personal and work relationships and can cause depression in children. He refutes the idea that expressing anger is healthier than suppressing it. He describes ways to control anger by inhibiting the three critical aspects of an angry reaction: thought, feelings, and action. He suggests that counting to 10 gives a person time to reinterpret what has happened by thinking, "Maybe he couldn't help it," or "There's no need to take it personally." The added time also allows one to become aware of emotions by noting, "My muscles are tense. Just relax." Finally, he suggests developing a few good lines to defuse situations, such as "Boy, you must be having a rough day" or "Yeah, that was pretty stupid of me." He details ways to control a number of negative emotions that make it very difficult to live and work with other people.

One of the most critical self-regulatory skills for students to cultivate is impulse control. In a famous experiment with 4-year old children in the late 1960s, Walter Mischel (2014) offered the children one marshmallow immediately, or two marshmallows if they could wait with the marshmallow in front of them while he went and did something else for 15 minutes. Only about 30% of the children could wait long enough to get the second marshmallow. Mischel discovered later that those kids who were able to delay their gratification when they were 4 years old went on to lead much more successful lives than the others. They were more popular with peers and teachers, earned higher salaries, and had a lower body mass index and less drug abuse. As Mischel characterized the difference, "If you can deal with hot emotions, then you can study for the SAT instead of watching television. And you can save more money for retirement. It's not just about marshmallows" (quoted in Lehrer, 2009).

The children who were successful at the task managed to distract themselves, such as by playing games under the table, so they could not see the marshmallow. Mischel discovered that he could teach kids how to succeed at impulse control by teaching them strategies for distracting or distancing themselves from temptations. With colleagues, he is now working with schools to teach children strategies they can use throughout their lives to exercise self-control. He teaches kids to recognize specific situations that trigger emotional reactions, and "if-then" strategies for coping with such situations. As he says, "Once you realize that willpower is just a matter of learning how to control your attention and thoughts, you can really begin to increase it" (quoted in Konnikova, 2014).

A recent book, *Willpower*, by Roy Baumeister and John Tierney (2011), describes Baumeister's research on self-control over 30 years. As Baumeister and Tierney declare, "Self-regulation failure is the major pathology of our time" (p. 11). They point to evidence that it contributes to high divorce rates, domestic violence, crime, and a host of other problems. Baumeister's studies found that willpower diminishes during the day as we grow hungrier and use up our strength to resist temptations.

It turns out that measures of self-control are a good predictor of a student's college grade point average, and in fact a better predictor than IQ or SAT scores. In workplaces, people high in self-control rate more favorably with their peers and their subordinates. They are better at empathizing and considering other people's perspectives, less prone to mental problems, and less likely to become angry or aggressive. This makes them much more productive in life.

As Baumeister and Tierney (2011) point out, the temptations in life have been getting stronger as we become surrounded by the delights of shiny goods and delicious foods. But they are optimistic that people can learn to cope better with all these temptations. Students need to learn to arrange their lives so they don't encounter so many temptations, just like the children who went under the table so they couldn't see the marshmallow. If you don't turn on the Home Shopping Network, you won't use up your self-control in resisting stuff you don't need. That is a metaphor for how to get the benefits that willpower brings.

By working to meet deadlines, students will need to learn to avoid distractions and focus their minds on getting their work done. By working with other students on projects, they will need to learn to control their emotions when they disagree about how to proceed. Creating schools that are collaborative work environments can teach many of the aspects of self-regulation that are critical for a successful life.

Planning, Monitoring, and Reflecting

To be strategic in life, students need to learn to be strategic about learning. Planning, monitoring, and reflecting are key to improving how one does anything, from solving problems to playing the piano. Planning involves thinking about what has worked in similar situations and how to apply those lessons to new situations. Monitoring involves observing whether one's plans are working, and correcting for any problems that arise. Reflecting involves looking back to determine what one could have done better and thinking about what skills and strategies one should work to improve.

President Dwight Eisenhower, who led the Allied forces in Europe during World War II, spent most of the war planning how to defeat the Germans. He made a famous observation: "Plans are worthless, but planning is everything" (1957). Military planners keep encountering new obstacles and problems as the plan unfolds, so they have to keep changing their plans. A plan may be a beginning, but to be successful, a person has to keep adapting it to fit the circumstances. Hence, it is adaptability in planning that wins wars—and life.

Psychologist Carol Dweck (2008) tells the story of a student who applied to only one graduate school and did not get in. To encourage a growth mindset, she asked the student to think what she could do to improve her chances in that future. Together, they worked out a plan to call a professor at the school to find out what the student could have done to make her application more successful. The student was scared, but she carried out the plan by calling the professor and explaining that she was not disputing the school's decision. Two days later, the professor called back and admitted the student to the program, impressed with her strategy and interest.

Not all plans are so successful, but Dweck (2008) emphasizes that making "vivid, concrete plans" is critical to succeeding in whatever endeavor a person decides to pursue. For students, it might be to complete an assignment, get more exercise, or discuss difficult issues with a friend. Dweck recommends addressing three questions:

1. *When* will you follow through on your plan?
2. *Where* will you do it?
3. *How* will you do it? (p. 228)

Dweck (2008) argues that these questions need to be addressed in vivid detail, which will dramatically improve the chances of follow-through and the chances of success. Students not only need a plan, but they need to visualize how to carry out the plan in a concrete way. For example, if they want to lose weight, they need to plan how to get sugars and junk food out of their house and life, so they aren't tempted to eat them. And they need to develop a plan to exercise, perhaps by going to the gym or getting up early each morning to run or walk. It must be something they enjoy! Joining a team or arranging to meet with a group for exercise helps ensure that they'll do it. Precisely specifying plans, as Dweck suggests, can help with follow-through. Students need to employ every possible strategy to make sure their plans succeed.

After most people start a task, they just keep doing what they started out to do without asking themselves how they are doing and if they are actually making progress toward their goals. Math professor Alan Schoenfeld (1985) taught a course where he asked students to work in groups to solve difficult math problems. He found at first that the groups would pick a strategy and pursue it without monitoring their progress at all. Sometimes they would simply flounder around, trying one move after another, not making any progress at all. He decided to rotate among the students asking three questions to make sure they were monitoring their work: "What are you trying to do? Why are you doing it? How will it help you solve the problem?" Addressing these questions forced students to articulate their reasons for what they were doing and helped them learn to ask themselves these questions in the future. Such self-monitoring in invaluable.

Schoenfeld (1985) argues that several control strategies for making executive decisions are critical to problem solving. These include generating alternative courses of action, evaluating which are most likely to succeed and which can most likely be carried out, and considering what heuristics might apply. Heuristics are rules of thumb for solving problems that can be helpful but are not guaranteed to work, such as breaking a problem into subproblems or making simplifying assumptions. Students can be taught to apply control strategies as they work through problems, especially whenever they encounter difficulties in making progress toward a solution.

Figuring out how they could have done work differently is critical to improving their work in the future. If schools are going to teach planning, monitoring, and reflecting, they have to engage students in substantive tasks that can benefit from these efforts. Students need to tackle issues they care about, carrying out projects and investigations that lead to products they can defend and be proud of. As they work on their projects, students should keep reflective journals on problems they encounter and how they dealt with them, as well as on what they learned and how they can work together better in the future (Kolodner et al., 2003; White & Frederiksen, 2005).

Becoming More Adaptive

The ultimate goal of teaching students to be strategic is to enable them to adapt to whatever life throws at them. Giyoo Hatano and Kayoko Inagaki (1986) first introduced the difference between routine expertise and adaptive expertise in differentiating between sushi cooks who expertly produce sushi according to the classic techniques and sushi cooks who have mastered the classic techniques but go on to invent new techniques of their own. Because the world is changing faster these days, it is more important than ever for young people to learn to be adaptive enough to cope with new challenges and opportunities. To be effective, students need to learn to recognize what people in their surroundings are thinking and the goals they are pursuing, as well as any obstacles or opportunities that have arisen. This involves students continually monitoring the situation for any changes or new insights into what is happening around them.

John Bransford and his colleagues (Bransford, Brown, & Cocking, 2000) suggest that an important component of adaptive expertise comes from how problems are framed. They tell the story of how tomato growers asked engineers to design an automatic picking machine that did not bruise the tomatoes. After many unsuccessful attempts at coming up with such a machine, biologists solved the problem by growing tomatoes with thicker skins—a creative reframing of the problem. Taking different perspectives on a problem can often lead to an alternative framing that solves the problem. It always pays to ask how a problem might be framed differently.

Bransford and colleagues (2000) argue that collecting information is critical to understanding the situation and coming up with novel solutions. Most people tend to act first and think later. Often they don't know what it is that they don't know—the "unknown unknowns," in Donald Rumsfeld's felicitous phrase about war. Students should be taught to pursue the underlying causes that led to a current state of affairs in order to develop the best framing of the problem and novel solutions. For example, if they are investigating the problem of computer game addiction, they might study the tricks that game designers use to keep players from going off to do other things as well as the methods used to treat addicts. This involves questioning assumptions and identifying sources of information that can help them think about the problem more effectively.

Extensive evidence shows we all learn best when we struggle to understand things (Kapur, 2008; Kapur & Bielaczyc, 2011; Stigler & Hiebert, 1999). Teachers know that it pays to connect new lessons to frameworks and experiences students have encountered in the past. One effective strategy for learning is to compare contrasting cases, such as the differences between work groups that were productive versus those that were unproductive (Bransford, Franks, Vye, & Sherwood, 1989). The differences between cases highlight critical features that learners should pay attention to as they try to make sense of a new problem or situation. This is the way scientists often construct their theories. In order to get children to develop a growth mindset, Carol Dweck (2008) teaches them that struggling with ideas helps build new connections in the brain. We can make ourselves smarter if we are willing to put in the effort to make sense of the world. If we don't put in the effort, we won't be able to adapt to new situations.

There is a lot students can do to make themselves smarter and more strategic—to become adaptive thinkers. They need to develop a growth mindset. They need to plan, monitor, and reflect on what they do. They need to consider multiple perspectives in order to frame problems and develop situation awareness. There is an endless variety of strategies to help accomplish all these things. Effective strategies are central to developing adaptive expertise. But they will never develop unless students are engaged in what they see as meaningful activities.

TOWARD SCHOOLING FOR SELF-RELIANCE

Managing health, finances, and legal issues are critical to survival in the changing economy, but K–12 schooling barely touches on these topics. Becoming a strategic thinker and learner who can adapt to the disruptions happening all around us is the only way to cope in a complex, changing society. Self-reliance is the only protection in the new economy. Ask yourself if schools are preparing students for this new world. Are schools emphasizing strategic thinking? Are they teaching robust financial understanding? Are they emphasizing adaptation to change? Are they helping students learn how to preserve their health and prevent illness? The answer to these questions is largely no. Research has learned much about these issues, but most of this knowledge has not filtered into a very crowded curriculum.

Schools can teach self-reliance if they involve students in accomplishing substantial pieces of work. Students can be asked to study and develop solutions to some of the major problems facing society. Ideally, these would be problems that students understand they are likely to face as they go out into the world. Hence, they will take the problems seriously and try to come up with solutions that have a chance to work. By having students work together and meet deadlines, they will be called upon to develop strategies to manage their work and meet expectations. And they will be forced to confront the serious issues they may face in the future.

CHAPTER 4

CAREER SKILLS FOR THE NEW ECONOMY

In his book *Where Good Ideas Come From*, Steven Johnson (2010) tells the story: "Sometime in the late 1870s, a Parisian obstetrician named Stephane Tarnier took a day off from his work at Maternité de Paris, the lying-in hospital for the city's poor women, and paid a visit to the nearby Paris Zoo. . . . Tarnier stumbled across an exhibit of chicken incubators. Seeing the hatchlings stumble about in the incubator's warm enclosure triggered an association in his head, and before long he had hired Odile Martin, the zoo's poultry raiser, to construct a device that would perform a similar function for human newborns" (p. 25).

Johnson argues that this is the way new ideas are hatched. Ideas and people come in contact and rub against one another, sparking new ideas. This is the kind of creativity in solving problems that is becoming central to success in the modern workplace. And yet, the traditional school provides little incentive or opportunity for cultivating such creativity. Most teachers value students who do what they are told and don't ask questions that challenge the way things are done. Good students don't go hatching ideas the teacher has never thought about before.

As technology has invaded the workplace, the demand for workers who can do routine jobs has decreased and the demand for workers who can think creatively has increased. For example, economists find that the percentage of the workforce engaged in routine jobs has fallen by about 8% since 2001, and that nonroutine jobs have increased by about 23% over the same period. The *Wall Street Journal* (Zumbrum, 2015) suggests, "Is your job routine? If so, it's probably disappearing."

Robots are increasingly doing many of the industrial jobs that workers once had to carry out. Sophisticated systems can read though masses of documents to find information needed for some purpose, such as finding relevant legal cases and making medical diagnoses. Automated cars and trucks and drones may soon pick up people and goods and take them to specified destinations.

For students to thrive in the workplace of the future—the future that is happening *now*—they must learn to be creative and critical thinkers. They must also master vital workplace skills, such as managing their time and resources and working effectively in teams with people from different cultures. These are skills that can't be automated—and they are essential to the thinking jobs the future holds. We will always need doctors and analysts and entertainers, even when the routine jobs disappear. But to earn a living wage in the new economy will require skills that today's schools are not effectively teaching. We can design schools to teach these new skills if we challenge kids to accomplish meaningful tasks, like designing new products and finding solutions to societal problems.

LEARNING FOR TOMORROW'S WORKPLACE

In their groundbreaking book *The Second Machine Age*, Eric Brynjolfsson and Andrew McAfee (2014) argue, "there's never been a worse time to be a worker with only 'ordinary' skills and abilities to offer, because computers, robots, and other digital technologies are acquiring these skills and abilities at an extraordinary rate" (p. 11). Industrial robots are already busy in many large manufacturing plants and warehouses, performing repetitive tasks and delivering goods. Eventually robots will be developed to monitor what other robots are doing and summon help if problems arise.

In February 2011, millions of Americans watched as the computer program Watson beat the two reigning champions, Ken Jennings and Brad Rutter, on the quiz program *Jeopardy!* (Markoff, 2011). This incident represents a high point in the development of artificial intelligence to date. As Ken Jennings said at the end of the program, "I, for one, welcome our new computer overlords" (quoted in Markoff, 2011). To answer a *Jeopardy!* question, Watson has to figure out what the question is asking, search a huge database that includes Wikipedia, retrieve the relevant information, form a large set of hypotheses as to a possible answer, and weigh them against one another to decide which answer is most likely and how certain it is of the answer.

Watson has a wide range of possible uses. With its medical database, it is being used for diagnosing cases of lung cancer. It is also being used to train new doctors in the diagnosis of medical problems. Because Watson can access all the information on the web for treating health problems, it has a much larger resource base to draw upon than any one doctor, given that the medical literature is huge and constantly growing. But Watson is also being used to support financial analysis and customer service. Systems like Watson are likely to play a major role in the future in any field where large amounts of information are being collected that go beyond human capability to fully process.

At present, computer systems that help customers make travel plans are replacing travel agents, and systems that do taxes are replacing tax consultants. The number of secretaries in corporations has diminished considerably as other employees use computers to do all their own work. More and more writers are publishing their own work in blogs and online books, thus bypassing the publishing industry. Soon, computer systems that can do research to find relevant legal cases on any topic will replace law clerks. Hardly any routine jobs are safe.

The jobs that *are* developing involve thinking and creativity, self-management, and the ability to work with all kinds of people. These jobs might involve troubleshooting or research, managing groups or designing new products, and using technical or communication skills more effectively. For example, farmers in the new economy do much more than grow crops. They calculate which crops will produce the most income, anticipate risks and deal with problems, hire workers and navigate complex government policies, negotiate with buyers, and purchase heavy equipment. Writers today must build a brand, decide which outlets will best help them find an audience, and develop contacts with people in the field who can help advance their career. Successful careers today require a variety of skills that schools barely touch upon.

Technology is changing at an ever-faster rate. Many of the best jobs in the future will involve designing, testing, and using new technologies. People will have to be savvy enough to adapt to the changing technological environment. Understanding both how technology works and its limitations is becoming more and more critical for success in our complex world. Today's students should be learning how to deal creatively with the changing nature of work.

As Tom Friedman (2004) dramatizes with his metaphor of a "flat world," people in the developed world are now competing for jobs with people in China, India, and other nations in the developing world. To thrive in this environment, it will not be enough to have a traditional liberal arts education where students learn about Shakespeare, the quadratic formula, plate tectonics, and the Industrial Revolution. Students also need marketable skills to earn a living wage in a hypercompetitive world. Nor will vocational education effectively prepare students with its focus on training for specific jobs, such as auto mechanics or wind-farm development—jobs that are likely to change drastically or disappear completely in the coming years. Neither tradition will save us.

New technologies are erasing the divide between education for elites and non-elites. Traditionally, liberal arts education was aimed at preparing elites to take their place as leaders in society. Similarly, vocational education was premised on the idea that many people in society were only qualified for routine work. As routine jobs disappear, we must figure out how to teach students the knowledge and skills that the world demands.

Can we teach students to be creative and critical thinkers? To manage their time and resources? To work effectively with other people? I think it is possible to do so, but most schools haven't tried. They have been so focused on testing how many facts and procedures students can memorize that they have largely neglected the critical knowledge and skills that the modern workplace demands. In this chapter, let's look at some of what future workers would do well to learn.

HOW CAN STUDENTS LEARN PRODUCTIVE THINKING?

Changes in technology and the skills needed for the modern workplace have dramatically increased the need for both creative and critical thinking. Whereas creative thinking involves generation of new ideas and products, critical thinking involves the evaluation of ideas and products. Both are equally important to productive thinking.

Creative Thinking

We want to foster students' creativity so they can thrive in the 21st-century workplace. But how does anyone "think creatively"? Some years ago, I conducted an experiment to find out how creative people come up with their ideas. I asked subjects to generate ideas for writing an essay on the topic "What Makes a Party Interesting." I recorded their thinking aloud and analyzed the different ways subjects approached the problem. The approaches taken by two participants nicely illustrate the kinds of strategies that creative thinkers use to develop new ideas and that students should be learning in school.

One participant was Dedre Gentner, a leading cognitive psychologist, who is famous for her work on how people recognize and understand analogies. She talked through four cases of parties she had attended in order to identify what differentiated the fun ones from the duds. She came up with two characteristics that psychologists refer to as "intermediate constructs" that seemed critical to a party's success. One was whether there were spaces she called "cover," where people could gather to have quiet conversations. The other characteristic involved "disruptive activities" that could provide an excuse for people to move on, such as dancing or getting drinks. These thoughts came from her memory of one ghastly party where everyone sat around in a circle and talked together: It was so bad, she felt obligated to talk so the conversation wouldn't die, and later the hostess criticized her for dominating the conversation.

After she identified cover and disruptive activities as key concepts, she began to construct a process model. In her idea of a fun party, people move around and talk to different people in the spaces where they find cover. Sometimes the conversations work well, and partygoers resist the activities that draw others out of boring conversations. The analogy she made is that an engrossing conversation, which holds people together, is like the precipitation of molecules in a chemical soup of moving particles.

In contrast, Oliver Selfridge, an early figure in the field of artificial intelligence and a writer of children's books, looked at parties via a strategy of perspective shifting that Richard Young, Alton Becker, and Kenneth Pike (1970) describe in their book *Rhetoric: Discovery and Change*. He considered parties throughout history and in different venues, and the different elements that constituted "parties." He even went into the derivation of the word *party* and what that implied about the essential aspects of parties. His final analysis consisted of a small set of critical elements that he considered necessary for an interesting party, such as intelligent discussion, provocative ideas, and amusing people. He treated these elements as primitives, analogous to the chemical elements.

Can students be taught to think with the creativity of a Dedre Gentner or Oliver Selfridge? Listening in on their thinking suggests a number of strategies that creative people use to come up with new ideas. These strategies can be taught to students who are engaged in working on creative projects where they are encouraged to come up with new ideas and solutions as they design, investigate, and construct meaningful products and arguments. For each strategy we suggest how students might learn to use the strategy effectively.

- *Compare cases.* Gentner compared parties that varied with respect to how interesting they were in order to determine what makes a party interesting. She chose parties that varied in how much fun they were. This allowed her to consider different factors that affected how interesting the party was. For any topic, it is critical to come up with a variety of cases that vary on critical dimensions to consider. For example, if students are analyzing the question "What makes a network business successful?," they need to examine both failures and successes across a variety of different contexts.
- *Consider near-misses.* By considering cases that failed in some way, Gentner identified critical factors that she might not have thought of otherwise. For example, she thought of a party where everyone gathered in a circle, which made it impossible for individuals to

move around or have intimate conversations. This case led her to the critical factors she developed. Considering a number of near-misses highlights the different factors that may be critical. When students are comparing cases, it is the near-misses that are perhaps most revealing, so they will want to look closely at cases that fail for different reasons.

- *Probe for critical factors.* Gentner looked for variables that lay below the superficial variables that anyone might notice about different parties, such as whether they served alcohol and how interesting the people were. This allowed her to come up with an innovative theory that few would think of. As students consider possible factors leading to business success, they should try to see what different cases have in common at a deeper level.

- *Look for an analogy.* In order to construct a coherent theory, Gentner made an analogy between people and molecules moving around in a chemical soup, where molecules can come together and precipitate out of the soup. Analogies often provide new insights that students might not think of otherwise. As they probe deeper, students should look for analogies that can provide a coherent structure to frame their understanding.

- *Consider different perspectives.* Young, Becker, and Pike (1970) suggest strategies to use in viewing a phenomenon from different angles. One strategy they suggest is to view the phenomenon as a *particle*, *wave*, or *field*. The *particle* view involves seeing the phenomenon as an isolated thing, highlighting its different features or subsystems. A house might be seen as painted brown, with a gabled roof and a front porch. The *wave* view suggests looking at the phenomenon as it has changed over time. The house might be viewed as originally a farmhouse built some hundred years earlier that was modernized as the suburbs grew up around it, with a wing added to provide an apartment for a grandmother. The *field* view involves viewing the phenomenon in context. The house might be surrounded by new large houses and set back from the street, with stone walls along the border where the farm ended and large hemlock trees shading it from the sun. These three perspectives can be applied recursively to different aspects of the phenomenon, probing deeper and wider as you think more about the topic. As students tackle a complex problem, they need to learn to come at the problem from different perspectives.

- *Develop a simulation.* Einstein was famous for his "thought experiments," such as where he imagined himself riding on a light beam in order to develop his theory of relativity. Simulation is a strategy for running a model of a phenomenon over time with different input conditions to see what happens. For example, students might imagine different scenarios of how society may change if everyone becomes a freelance worker. Simulation gives one the possibility to consider alternative worlds where things are very different.

- **Identify a target structure.** Selfridge tried to identify the primitive elements, akin to the chemical elements, that were necessary to create an interesting party. This idea of primitive elements was the structure he used to guide his thinking. The structure guiding Gentner's theory building was a process model, where elements (that is, people) interact with one another when they come into contact. This kind of process model, called an "agent model," is common in artificial intelligence (Wilensky & Reisman, 2006). Students will do well to practice developing their own theories, given the kinds of structures (or model types) described in Chapter 6.

In his book *The Creative Attitude*, Roger Schank (1988), a leading artificial intelligence researcher, advocates creating theories to explain anomalies, checking theories with data, and making generalizations:

> The trick for the creative person is to identify those things that do not work and to begin to think about them. What does this mean in actual practice? It means wondering why the buses don't run on time and seem to bunch up in groups. It means thinking about how tipping actually influences service and how the system could be improved. It means wondering how well intelligence is measured by IQ tests and trying to think about what intelligence actually is. . . . In order to find a solution for a puzzling problem, one cannot wait to be presented with the puzzling problem by someone else. You must think of the problem yourself. . . . But in order to think up good problems, one must notice anomalies. (p. 350)

How can we teach students to be more creative in everyday life? Having students develop solutions for serious problems such as how to improve the coordination between schooling and careers or how to develop effective work groups will encourage students to come up with creative ideas. Theorizing involves trying to make sense of the way things work, like the 2-year-old who wants to know why things are the way they are. School-age children often begin to lose that sense of wonder as they go through school. Ken Robinson (2010) suggests that school beats it out of them. The trick is getting students to regain this questioning attitude with more critical insight.

Critical Thinking

As the world of work becomes more competitive, there is more and more emphasis on developing the most effective work processes (Hammer & Hershman, 2010). Workers need to question the way things have always been done in order to come up with better ways to do things. They need to try out new ideas and evaluate how well they work. They need to tackle problems when things go wrong and figure out how to solve them. Critical thinking turns up in every corner of the modern workplace.

Evaluation is the essence of critical thinking. What gets evaluated in a work product? We can critique its content, style, rationale, creativity, and structure, as well as the processes involved in producing the work. Many different work processes can be examined, such as problem solving, designing, writing, speaking, performing, and decisionmaking. Two major goals of evaluating are to improve the product and similar products in the future, and to improve the way products are produced.

For example, Barbara White and John Frederiksen (1998) had students evaluate their group science projects in terms of nine criteria, organized into three categories:

- Broad criteria
  - » Understanding the science
  - » Understanding the process of inquiry
  - » Making connections
- More focused criteria
  - » Being inventive
  - » Being systematic
  - » Using the tools of science
  - » Reasoning carefully
- Socially oriented criteria
  - » Writing and communicating well
  - » Teamwork

After students evaluated the research they had just completed, they were asked to write a justification for their score on each criterion. Students who did these evaluations produced research projects that were more highly rated by independent observers than students in control classes. They also scored higher on tests of their learning. This reflective evaluation was particularly beneficial for low-achieving students.

In evaluating content, two of the key questions students need to learn to ask are: Have important ideas been left out, and is all of the material included necessary? Students leave out important ideas either because they don't think of them or because they assume they aren't needed. The trouble with including too much is that the important ideas may get lost in the jumble. Asking these two questions is central to critiquing both one's own work and others' work.

Diane Halpern (1998) cites extensive evidence that critical thinking can be learned. In working with students, she has developed a four-part program to becoming a critical thinker. The four parts include: (1) a disposition to engage in critical thinking, (2) instruction and practice with critical thinking skills, (3) structure-training activities designed to facilitate transfer across domains, and (4) a strategic component used to direct and assess thinking.

In their book *The Five Elements of Effective Thinking*, Edward Burger and Michael Starbird (2013) suggest strategies that can help students become critical thinkers. One way to deepen understanding is to try to explain one's own work to others. Burger and Starbird asked a math teacher when he learned calculus, and he said it was when he tried to teach it: "When I try to teach something, I have to confront many fundamental questions: What is the motivation to learn this topic? What are the basic examples? On what aspects of this material should I focus? What are the underlying themes? What ties the ideas together? What is the global structure? What are the important details? These questions force me to discover the heart of the matter, and see exactly what I truly understand and what I still need to work on" (p. 80). Engaging students in teaching others is a powerful way for them to learn (Heath & Mangiola, 1991).

In Burger's college math class, he would appoint an "official questioner" for the day. One girl, when she was the questioner, reflected that she was "more aware of what went on, and more attuned to the subtler content of the discussion. She also admitted that she got more out of class." She became a regular question-poser after that. As Burger and Starbird (2013) argue:

> With practice you can learn to take personal responsibility to understand what is being said as it happens in real time, and to actively construct questions about what is missing, what is assumed, what might be extended, and what is vague or unclear. If you embrace these habits of mind—forcing yourself to create and ask questions when you are listening to a lecture or anything else—you will find there are at least two effects: one, you will perform better; and, two, you will find the world more engaging. (p. 85)

How can we create classrooms where every student becomes a habitual "question-poser"? It is very productive to become a questioner about many aspects and situations of life. This means asking about goals and purposes and about costs and benefits. Students become more alive and curious because they are actively engaged. They become more open to ideas because they are questioning their assumptions. And they take more effective action because they clarify what needs to be done. Questioning pays off in many ways.

In solving problems, developing designs, or making diagnoses, today's employees must often make difficult decisions that require critical thinking. Students are faced with making important life decisions, such as what career to pursue, which college to go to, or what job to take. These are decisions that involve cost-benefit analysis.

For example, suppose you are considering two possible colleges, one in Southern California near the beach and one in the Boston area. The one in Boston has a very good reputation, with many distinguished alumni. On the other hand, the one in California is in a warm climate and surfing is your favorite sport, though the school's reputation is as more of a party school. Cost-benefit analysis dictates that you should look at all the pros and cons of each choice: The benefits for California might be a more relaxed atmosphere, warmer climate, surfing, and better health. The costs might be less interesting classes and people, less productivity, and less mentoring. Costs and benefits for Boston would be the inverse of the California benefits and costs. Weighing them, you might decide that the college in Boston is the better choice for your career, because hard work and mentoring are critical to a successful career, and if you are successful, you can always move to California later.

The kinds of strategies used in doing cost-benefit analysis are common to many other kinds of decision making, such as helping clients analyze problems and designing products, documents, and experiments. All such problems involve careful consideration of alternatives, and the pros and cons of each choice. Part of the skill of decision making involves knowing when to carry out in-depth analysis and when to cut the process short and rely instead on one's intuitive sense of the best choice.

Critical thinking takes work, but it is central to rational decision making. Diane Halpern (1998) has shown that we can teach critical thinking and questioning. It is best taught in the context of students engaged in tasks that they find challenging and meaningful. Chapter 7 discusses how school can be redesigned to engage children in doing projects that involve the strategies of creative and critical thinking that people can use in their work and their lives.

HOW CAN STUDENTS LEARN
TO MANAGE TIME, RESOURCES, AND GROUP-WORK?

In the modern workplace, people are facing many demands on their time that they must manage and a glut of information they must keep track of. Further, in more and more careers, they are required to work with a wide variety of people to solve problems and complete projects. Students need to learn how to cope with these kinds of demands when they are in school, rather than confronting them for the first time when they take a job.

Managing Time

The fundamental time-management problem that skilled workers face is meeting deadlines on the projects in which they engage. Some projects may be solo efforts, but most involve working with others and fulfilling expectations that some piece of the work will be completed on time. The structure of school, with its emphasis on individual work and short tasks, does not foster the learning of robust time-management skills.

To learn time management, students need to work on long-term projects they care about with tight deadlines. They need to learn about planning their time, estimating realistically how long different jobs will take, and coordinating work with other students. This often involves checking in at regular intervals to see if each person involved in a project is on track to finish his or her work on time. Even on solo projects, checking progress is critical. When things fall behind, there is a need to replan in order to allocate part of the work to someone else or to find a work-around that makes it possible to complete the project by the deadline. Students need a lot of practice to develop these skills.

A common time-management problem, particularly among young people, involves multitasking. When working or studying, students are often interrupted by text messages, emails, or phone calls, which force them to switch from what they are doing to processing the interruption. As Larry Rosen (2010) discusses in his book *Rewired*, there is a time cost for switching tasks, as well as recovery time when people go back to what they were doing—they have to figure out where they were when they were interrupted. Even more costly is the fact that the interruption provides an opportunity to do other things, like checking for Facebook updates or getting a snack. There may be no way to cure students of multitasking, because they are driven by a fear of missing an important message and being left out. But it is much better to handle incoming messages through batch processing at periodic intervals: handling all text messages, emails, or phone calls every hour or two, rather them letting them interrupt tasks. Students will only learn this by working to meet deadlines.

In three studies comparing people who frequently engaged in multitasking with those who did not, Eyal Ophir, Clifford Nass, and Anthony Wagner (2009) found that frequent multitaskers were easily distracted by irrelevant stimuli and slower to switch from one task to another as compared to infrequent multitaskers. We are producing a generation of young people who think they are good at multitasking, when all the evidence shows they are no better than anyone else.

Procrastination is another source of time-management problems. We all put off what we don't want to do, though some of us are more persistent than others. Students should learn not to put off starting tasks until it is too late to do a good job. How can this habit be broken? One strategy for combating students' procrastination is to pick a time of day, such as the morning or after a meal, when their willpower is greatest to tackle tasks that they have been putting off. Studies by Baumeister and Tierney (2011) show that willpower diminishes during the day as we grow hungrier and use up our strength to resist temptations. Students need to learn to make a specific plan for accomplishing the task, as Dweck (2008) suggests, whenever they catch themselves procrastinating.

Many people start things they never finish. Often, this results from poor planning, distraction, or perfectionism. The source of perfectionism is fear of criticism, which has been internalized into self-criticism (Guise, 2015). Perfectionism is hard to cure, because it is deeply rooted. The most effective strategy to replace perfectionism is "satisficing"—that is, doing a good enough job, given the importance of the task. This can involve doing very little because the task does not matter much, or striving hard because it matters quite a lot. The myth about the Nobel Prize winner Herbert Simon, who invented the term *satisficing*, was that he ate the same sandwich every day for lunch because he didn't much care what he ate. But if a task matters a lot, then it is important to finish the job. The trouble is that perfectionists tend to strive for perfection in everything.

Another reason people fail to complete tasks is that they don't plan their time well enough to do everything by the deadline. Individuals differ in regard to how much "time urgency" they feel and whether they are "present oriented" or "future oriented" (Waller, Conte, Gibson, & Carpenter, 2001). People with strong "time urgency" worry much more about time passing than those who don't much pay attention to the passage of time. People who are "future oriented" make plans for the future, in contrast to those who focus on the present. Waller and her colleagues suggest that a future orientation combined with a sense of time urgency is critical to organizing activity to meet future deadlines. Students need to be taught how to organize their time to meet deadlines. Teachers can help them set priorities so that the most critical pieces of work are done early in the process. There is a tendency to "downslide" into meeting the most immediate demands rather than focusing on the most critical tasks. Monitoring one's own and others' work is the only way to prevent this kind of downsliding. This involves regular check-ins, where everyone reports on their progress, or having the group leader check regularly with people to see how their work is going.

It will often be necessary to reallocate time and effort as a task proceeds. As pointed out in Chapter 3, planning is never finished. Students need to monitor how their work is going and replan as necessary. Just the act of monitoring and replanning helps them learn to be more realistic in their planning. Finally, they need to reflect on the process when they're done. A reflective discussion allows them to objectively consider how they could have planned the work better. To learn these skills, students must work in groups, structured so they engage in planning, monitoring, and reflecting. These are all vital skills for working in the kinds of teams that pervade modern corporations.

Getting Organized

The fundamental problem in organizing materials involves deciding what is worth saving versus what should be thrown away, as well as what is worth getting in the first place. This is the essential dilemma of being organized. The general rule is to obtain only what you will use and get rid of what you're not likely to need later. Students need to learn early on how to keep things organized or their lives will slowly fill with clutter. Learning how to index things and resist the urge to accumulate are important lessons.

In recent years, computers and the Internet have entered the organizational fray. In principle, they should make searching easier, because of multiple indexing. For example, one can search Google for relevant articles by typing in "meeting deadlines in group-work." Computer files can be multiply indexed, so there is less need to throw anything away, unless the system is running out of storage space. Rather than pruning, it is easier to buy more storage space, which is pretty cheap. As we store more information in cyberspace, we are beginning to accumulate less paper.

One good way for students to learn organizational skills is to keep an online portfolio of all their work on different projects over their school years, including both projects for school and projects out of school. Such a portfolio and the supporting documents students gather will accumulate over the years, as their skills slowly develop for indexing and searching the materials they collect. If students are producing various kinds of work products, such as in the Digital Youth Network described in Chapter 2, then teachers should encourage them to organize and index the works they produce over time, so that other students can see their works and critique them.

As students grow up in a digital world, they may learn how to use their devices to keep track of their work and their schedule. One advantage of smartphones is that they can remind people when they have something scheduled. Ideally, all the digital devices that students are growing up with will make it much easier for people to organize their lives more effectively. But students will have to learn to use these new capabilities to organize the stuff they collect and the appointments they make.

Working with Others

Work is becoming more collaborative as our society grows more complex. Teams are the critical unit in the workplace of the future. Working with others is being recognized as a sine qua non for success in the modern world. For example, as I pointed out in Chapter 1, working with others was highlighted in the SCANS report put together by the U.S. Department of Labor in an attempt to project what skills would be needed for the workplace of the future (SCANS Commission, 1991).

Psychologist Kevin Dunbar (1993) studied how researchers in four molecular biology laboratories do their work. By recording all the interactions in the labs, he was able to study idea generation in real settings. His most striking finding turned out to be the location where most of the important breakthroughs occurred. It was in lab meetings as researchers presented their most recent findings and problems. Other researchers who were working on related topics might help them interpret their findings or encourage the presenters to think about their work in a different way. Sometimes co-workers would suggest ways around problems that arose in experiments or provide reinterpretations of why the presenters were having a problem. Harnessing different viewpoints is critical to progress in more than just science; it is critical in every field and every endeavor. This kind of regular reporting on progress could be a very useful addition to classroom work.

Many companies have been putting together teams from across the company, such as from marketing, engineering, and manufacturing, in order to design more successful products, improve work processes, and do strategic planning (Brooks, 1994). But the members of these cross-functional teams come from different cultures with very different values, which often makes it difficult for team members to work together.

Anne Donnellon (1995) studied cross-functional product development teams in four different companies, including Xerox and Disney, and in three of the companies, the teams did not live up to their potential. Similarly, Ann Brooks (1994) studied four cross-functional teams in a large high-tech firm, which had similar problems. Companies are creating these teams with little effort to train their workers how to function well in teams. The one team that Donnellon (1995) found to live up to its potential was in a company division that made efforts to train its employees in teamwork and developed a culture that valued the products of team efforts.

Donnellon (1995) identifies six issues that are critical to the success of teams: (1) identification with the group, (2) interdependence, (3) power equity, (4) social closeness, (5) conflict management, and (6) effective negotiation. These six issues relate to critical capabilities that students need to develop in order to work successfully in groups. Everyone in a group needs to work to manage these six issues, because teams are fraught with tensions. Students can learn these skills as they work on group projects in school (Barron, 2000, 2003; Cohen, 1994) in the following ways:

1. Developing a group identity that team members share takes effort, and everyone must contribute. By working toward common goals and sharing expertise, a sense of "who we are" develops. The group language should emphasize "we" and "our," rather than "you" and "they."

2. Interdependence refers to members bringing their diverse knowledge and expertise together to solve problems as they arise. This requires respect for one another's ideas and points of view (Bielaczyc & Collins, 1999; Bielaczyc, Kapur, & Collins, 2013). Asking questions and listening carefully are important skills for fostering interdependence.

3. Both Brooks (1994) and Donnellon (1995) describe how power differences can undermine the success of groups. Groups must work to establish equity among different members or the contributions of lower-status members will be lost. White and Frederiksen (2005) achieve equal status through assigning a managerial role to each group member (see Chapter 2). The language for establishing equity requires everyone to avoid dominating the discussion, interrupting others, giving demands and directives, challenging others, and changing the topic.

4. In order to build team cohesion and prevent power differentiation, it is useful to use language to promote closeness among team members. As Donnellon (1995) argues, language to promote social closeness includes emphasizing common views and group membership, displays of concern for others' needs, acknowledging and responding to others' comments, and expressions of liking, admiration, empathy, and humor.

5. Conflict management is crucial to a team's success. There are many ineffective ways to resolve conflicts, such as leaders pushing their own ideas or members giving up their views in favor of others. The more effective ways of managing conflicts are through compromise and collaboration. As Donnellon (1995) says, "Collaboration can provide the basis for integration, by surfacing differences and discovering overlapping interests" (p. 38).

6. Developing effective negotiation strategies is critical to
    working with others. Donnellon (1995) distinguishes a win-
    lose orientation, which focuses on competition, from a win-
    win orientation, which focuses on collaboration. Effectively
    negotiating differences, as described in Chapter 2, is critical to
    bringing out and integrating the group's best ideas.

Schools need to develop student leaders who know how to get groups
to function effectively together. They have to feel a responsibility to connect
people with others and their ideas. They must learn how to inspire others
to set goals and work together to achieve those goals. They must learn how
to distribute work within the group to those most able to do the various
tasks. They must learn how to forge consensus among group members with
diverse views and expertise. And they must learn how to do all these things
while listening to others and sharing responsibility with them. The approach
of having students play managerial roles in their group-work, as described
in Chapter 2, is an effective way to teach students the kind of leadership
skills that are critical for effective group functioning.

The skills to work effectively with others are becoming more important
as the tasks we take on become more complex. No one person knows how
to turn out products like a cellphone or a car. These items have too many
sophisticated parts that suppliers often provide. It is teams that design such
products, figure out how to manufacture them, and develop plans to market
them. Teaching the kinds of skills that Donnellon (1995) and Brooks (1994)
have identified can enable students to learn how to work effectively with
others in today's workplace.

BUILDING SKILLS STUDENTS CAN USE IN FUTURE WORK

In this and other chapters, I describe a number of skills, strategies, and
dispositions that are critical to becoming a successful worker in the kinds
of workplaces that are emerging in a technology-based world. And yet, this
kind of knowledge is hardly touched upon in K–12 education. Do schools
teach students how to think critically and creatively? Do schools teach students how to prioritize what they do and manage their time and resources?
Do schools teach students how to work effectively in teams? For the most
part, the answer is no. The challenge for educators is to think about how to
design an education system that prepares students for the highly technological yet collaborative workplaces they will be entering.

CHAPTER 5

PUBLIC POLICY CHALLENGES

In her book *Thinking in Systems*, Donella Meadows (2008) argues: "Hunger, poverty, environmental degradation, chronic disease, drug addiction, and war, for example, persist in spite of the analytical ability and technical brilliance that have been directed toward eradicating them. No one deliberately creates these problems, no one wants them to persist, but they persist nevertheless. This is because they are inherently system problems— undesirable behaviors characteristic of the system structures that produce them. They will yield only as we reclaim our intuition, stop casting blame, see the system as the source of its own problems, and find the courage and wisdom to *restructure* it" (p. 4).

In our increasingly complex society, we are facing difficult policy challenges, such as climate change, pollution, and government finance, that require greater public understanding. The issues have grown more difficult to solve as the technologies and the systems that societies develop become more complex and change more rapidly. Learning to weigh the costs and benefits of different policies and consider possible risks are critical skills needed for active citizens to make wise policy decisions. Often, citizens and politicians do not understand complex issues well enough to debate them sensibly and base their decisions on the best possible evidence. For a society to function well, people must become much better informed about the complex trade-offs involved in making policy. Students need to learn about the trade-offs involved in environmental, governmental, and financial systems, as well as the basic concepts of systems theory. Schools often touch on these topics, but they do not approach them from the perspective of complex systems with feedback loops and leverage points.

UNDERSTANDING COMPLEX SYSTEMS

We are surrounded by complex systems, such as environmental systems, economic systems, medical systems, educational systems, and political systems. Meadows (2008) introduces several key ideas about system behavior.

First is the critical role of *feedback* in systems, and the use of negative feedback to control the behavior of systems. She tells the story of how the U.S. government mandated in 1986 that any corporation releasing hazardous pollutants must report those emissions publicly every year. This led to a 40% reduction in the amount of pollutants emitted, because companies did not want a reputation for polluting the air. This is an example of a high *leverage point* in the system.

She also discusses the notion of the *tragedy of the commons*, an idea that Garret Hardin (1968) introduced to explain a fundamental problem that occurs in any system where there are public goods that people share. For example, fisheries are shared resources that anyone can exploit, unless rules are set up to restrict their use. In market systems, as economist and philosopher Adam Smith argued, the price of goods provides feedback to the system, so that if the price rises, it encourages more people to provide the goods. But as Meadows points out, a *positive feedback loop* is set up where decreasing *stocks* of fish lead to increases in price, which in turn leads to overfishing, ending in the collapse of fish stocks.

Positive feedback loops are the source of many problems in systems. Meadows (1999) points to examples: "The more people catch the flu, the more they infect other people. The more babies are born, the more people grow up to have babies. The more soil erodes, the less vegetation it can support, the fewer roots and leaves to soften rain and runoff, the more soil erodes" (p. 11). Most efforts to control systems involve finding ways to prevent positive feedback loops from running wild. Doing this requires finding effective ways to intervene to break the loops.

As societies and their problems become more complex, it becomes more and more important for students to understand systems thinking. People often come up with solutions with side effects that make the problems worse. Politicians grab onto simple solutions because they are easy to sell to their constituents. As George Washington and Thomas Jefferson argued, we need a wise citizenry to debate issues sensibly and choose effective leaders. Given the growing complexity of problems, citizens need to choose leaders who think deeply about issues and who understand complex systems.

For students to come to understand the behavior of complex systems, they need to address the kinds of societal problems that Meadows raises in the introductory paragraph in this chapter. They might investigate such problems such as: How can we address the problem of drug addiction? What should we do to reduce the use of fossil fuels? How can we provide jobs for everyone, given that technology is replacing workers? What can we do to make it possible for everyone to earn a living? Investigating such serious problems will help students understand the difficulties in finding solutions to complex issues.

There are many reasons to ask students to investigate complex societal problems. Foremost among them is that the face validity of such problems provides strong motivation for students to think deeply and defend the approaches they think are most likely to be successful. Solving such problems requires students to develop an understanding of medical, economic, governmental, and environmental processes. Furthermore, these are systemic problems, so students must integrate knowledge from multiple disciplines. They are the kinds of problems that bring home critical aspects of systems thinking, such as leverage points, feedback loops, and incentives.

Groups of students can work together on these problems, where they explore the Internet to find relevant information, share their knowledge, listen to one another, generate alternative ideas, consider the costs and benefits of different approaches, and work to produce effective solutions. They can develop their solutions as presentations to other students and as position papers that justify their proposed solutions. This approach derives from problem-based learning (Barrows & Tamblyn, 1980; Hmelo-Silver, 2004). Such problems would teach collaboration, communication, design, and investigative skills.

This approach is very different from the "mile wide and inch deep" approach to education that the assessment system has fostered in K–12 schools. If we want students to care about what they are learning, and come away with more than a superficial understanding of scientific issues, they need to delve deeply into topics that are important and that they care about. I discussed health in Chapter 3, and below I take up the environmental and economic issues that students need to address as they carry out their investigations.

WHICH ENVIRONMENTAL ISSUES SHOULD STUDENTS LEARN ABOUT?

Environmental science brings together elements of the biological, physical, and social sciences in a context that matters greatly for the future of the world. Hence, it is an ideal context in which to introduce scientific thinking as a way to approach real-world problems. The issues raised below are all problems that students should investigate. Schools would do well to embed science education in contexts that students can see have important implications for their future.

As the world's population increases, environmental issues loom larger and larger. The environment is a complex system, which requires facility in systems thinking to understand—and this facility is largely missing from both the adult population and the school curriculum. If children are to prepare for an increasingly complex world, they need to begin to investigate how a complex system like the environment operates.

Population Growth

Students need to investigate how the growing population impacts the environment and whether the future population can be sustained. Because current estimates are that world population will grow from about 7.4 billion now to a peak of near 11 billion by the end of the century, it will be particularly important for tomorrow's citizens and leaders to prevent the growing population from using up resources, producing waste and pollution, and destroying plants and animals as well as their habitats.

Students should consider how the world will feed 11 billion people over the coming centuries, when our agricultural practices have undesirable side effects. Students should investigate the effects of the Green Revolution, aquaculture, and genetic modification on human health and the environment. They also should investigate how farming practices might be improved to reduce the effects of pesticides, fertilizers, antibiotics, hormones, water use, and soil erosion on the environment and human health. Students need to understand the trade-offs involved in dealing with these complex problems.

Critical Resources

Students should investigate which resources are running out and how the world can cope with the problems that may arise. In 1980, economist Julian Simon offered a bet to environmentalist Paul Ehrlich (1971), who had written in his book *Population Bomb* that the increasing population was using up Earth's resources in an unsustainable manner. Simon (1980) argued that over the past 100 years, the prices of most resources had fallen, when adjusted for inflation, despite the growing population. He argued that because of new sources, substitution of one resource for another (for example, using plastics instead of wood and metal), and new techniques for extracting resources, supply was growing faster than demand, and hence, prices were falling. The wager he offered was for Ehrlich to pick any raw material and a date more than 1 year away. If the price went up, Ehrlich would win the bet, and if the price went down, Simon would win. Ehrlich picked five metals (copper, chromium, nickel, tin, and tungsten) and 10 years as the time period. Ehrlich lost on all five bets when inflation was taken into account. But that is not the final word on resource depletion, because some of those metals are now higher in price.

One important resource that is endangered is fresh water, because of droughts and the depletion of underground aquifers. The depletion of water is an example of the tragedy of the commons (Hardin, 1968), because it is a common resource where different users compete to get as much water as they can. The situation requires government to allocate water fairly and efficiently.

Students should investigate whether resources, such as metals, water, and topsoil, are being used up. Because scientists such as Paul Ehrlich and Julian Simon have opposing positions on whether we are running out of critical resources, students need to consider such conflicting claims and draw their own conclusions about how governments should address these issues.

The most critical resource to be concerned about is energy. Students should study the costs and benefits of different energy sources, and in particular the pollution they cause and their effect on climate. They should learn the distinction between renewable sources, such as wind and solar energy, and nonrenewable sources, such as fossil fuels, and investigate the difficulties of moving from nonrenewable to renewable sources. For example, they should analyze how to deal with the fact that wind and solar are intermittent sources. Students might develop plans for mitigating the bad effects of different energy sources, and develop projections for energy needs in the future and how the relative use of different energy sources will change.

Pollution

Students should investigate the different kinds of pollution countries have faced in the past and the different solutions countries have developed to address those problems. One of the first versions of the pollution story occurred in Great Britain, which fueled its Industrial Revolution with its ample supplies of coal, which were used to run factories and heat people's homes. Coal use resulted in the killer London smog of 1952, where more than 100,000 people suffered respiratory ailments and 12,000 people died. Great Britain slowly weaned itself off coal, finally closing its last mine in 2008. A similar story happened with the River Thames, which flows through London. It was one of the most polluted rivers in the world, and by 1957, it was declared biologically dead. After cleanup, today it teems with wildlife. China and India are now trying to deal with the kind of extreme pollution that the developed world faced in the last century.

Students should study why industrializing countries create so much pollution, and how that creates a pressure from the population for the government to deal with pollution. This simple negative feedback loop is pervasive around the world. Students should also investigate what new kinds of pollution are occurring (such as carbon dioxide) and develop plans for coping with these new problems.

Species Extinction

Biologist E. O. Wilson (2003) estimated that if current rates of human destruction of the biosphere continue, half of all species on Earth will be extinct in 100 years. People have been killing off animals ever since humankind first arrived on the scene. Shortly after people first got to North and South America, many of the large animals disappeared. Species of horses, camels, bears, lions, mammoths, and mastodons were eliminated. And we are still at it. In fact, we are now killing off many plant species by cutting down rain forests.

Students should study which species are endangered and which species people have already destroyed. They can investigate what human actions lead to extinction, what measures are being taken to protect species, the successes and failures, and the trade-offs in trying to save different species. They can also develop plans to preserve some of the species that are endangered.

Climate Change

Students should study the history of Earth's climate and the factors that cause it to warm and cool. The history of the climate can be read from ice cores drilled in the ice pack of Greenland and Antarctica (Stager, 2011). For most of the planet's history, Earth was quite warm. The dinosaurs thrived in a world that was much warmer than it is today. In the warmest times, the carbon dioxide levels were higher and the sea level was over 200 feet higher than it is today. Starting some 30 million years ago, carbon dioxide levels fell, leading to an Ice Age that began 2 million years ago. During that time, the ice advanced for long stretches of time, covering large parts of Europe and North America, including the northern half of what is now the United States. These events were interrupted for relatively short stretches of time, when the ice receded during a period called an interglacial. We are currently living in an interglacial period that started 11,000 years ago. The large release of carbon dioxide and methane from burning fossil fuels will prevent the ice from returning anytime soon.

Students should investigate how greenhouse gases cause the Earth to warm, the different side effects warming has on the oceans, and the feedback loops that govern the climate system. They can project how different levels of carbon dioxide in the atmosphere will affect sea levels, and the effects of a rising sea level on living patterns around the world. They can also investigate what kinds of actions can be taken to mitigate the effects of climate change, and which effects cannot be reduced.

WHICH ECONOMIC ISSUES SHOULD STUDENTS LEARN ABOUT?

Understanding economics is critical both to making wise policy decisions and managing one's personal finances. For that reason, I argue that economics, along with environmental and health science, is crucial for everyone who lives in a complex society to understand. As in environmental science, in economics the world faces many serious issues that require systems thinking, because of the complex interaction of feedback loops and incentives. The issues discussed below are important problems that students should investigate.

Recessions, Depressions, Bubbles, and Booms

Students need to learn about the business cycle and the causes of economic booms and busts if they are going to demand wise policy decisions from their leaders. Misunderstandings about the economy are rampant; in fact, many politicians do not understand basic economics, such as how the money supply fluctuates. Both politicians and the populace in general need to be much better educated about these issues. Hence, we need to prepare students better to understand how the economic system works.

Milton Friedman won the Nobel Prize in 1976 in part for his studies of the causes of the Great Depression of the 1930s. He found that from the time of the Wall Street collapse in 1929 until 1933, the amount of money in circulation fell by 27%, an enormous decrease that led to an unemployment rate of over 20% in 1933 (Friedman & Schwarz, 1963). The decrease in the money supply was caused by the failure of banks. Banks create money by taking in deposits and lending out money based on those deposits. The winding down of banks and their loans in the Great Depression reversed this effect, causing enormous damage to economies around the world. Knowledge of what led to the Great Depression in 1929 enabled governments during the economic downturn in 2008 to take steps to prevent the collapse of financial institutions and the money supply, in order to prevent another depression. Students need to learn how important it is to protect financial institutions.

Students should also understand the causes of inflation. During booms, people and businesses are optimistic about the future. So people take out loans to buy goods, such as cars and houses, and businesses take out loans to make investments to increase their production. Inflation is brought about by businesses raising prices, which they can do when there is a lot of demand for their goods. When prices rise, workers demand wage increases so they can afford to pay the increased prices. This leads to a positive feedback loop, where businesses increase prices to pay higher wages, while workers demand ever-higher wages to pay the increased prices. To break this loop, central banks raise interest rates, which often leads to recession. Students should investigate how governments control the rate of inflation by varying interest rates.

Historically, economic bubbles have occurred periodically. The most famous one occurred in the 1630s in Holland, when tulips were first grown and the price rose dramatically, driven by speculators. At the peak of tulip mania, some tulip bulbs sold for more than 10 times the annual income of a skilled craftsman. When the bubble burst, as was inevitable, it had a devastating effect on many speculators and on the entire Dutch economy. The housing bubble in the United States that caused the 2008 financial crisis is a more recent example of how economic bubbles occur. Students should investigate how countries can develop measures to prevent bubbles from happening, rather than trying to cope with them after they burst.

Students need to investigate the causes of depressions, recessions, booms, and bubbles, and how governments and central banks have responded to them. They should investigate what policies have been put in place to reduce swings in the economy and how effective they have been. Furthermore, students should investigate how governments can most effectively prevent depressions and bubbles in the future.

Government Debt

Public debt and personal debt are very different, so it is important for students to learn the differences. People have to pay off their debts or go bankrupt, which can have nasty consequences. Governments, on the other hand, almost never pay off their debts, and that's not a bad thing. Governments may reduce their debt from time to time, but in general, the debt just keeps growing as the country's production of goods grows.

Students need to learn that deficit spending is needed during recessions and depressions to counter the decrease in the money supply, to cushion the impact of recessions on people, and to help the economy start growing. Since the Great Depression in the 1930s, developed countries have enacted a number of automatic countercyclical mechanisms that act to cushion the blow, such as unemployment compensation that rises during recessions, deposit insurance that pays people when banks fail, and increased deficit spending when receipts fall faster than spending.

The functions and dangers of government debt are not well understood by the public, which can lead to unwise policies. Students should study the history of government debt in different countries and how debt crises have been handled. They should track how government debt has varied in different eras and what factors have caused it to grow and decline. They should examine government and International Monetary Fund (IMF) policies for dealing with debt crises in different countries.

How Markets Function

The law of supply and demand is central to understanding the economy. Students need to understand how the market acts like an "invisible hand," guiding people and companies to produce those goods and services that are most in demand. They should also understand that although markets serve to allocate effort and resources efficiently, they don't take into account some of the costs of producing items, such as the cost of companies dumping their waste into rivers. Even beyond environmental costs, there are costs markets don't take into account. When a company lays off workers, it costs governments in terms of a loss of tax revenue and payment of unemployment benefits. It costs workers in terms of financial and social stress. When a company closes a factory, it leads to loss of taxes and increasing blight in the factory's neighborhood. Because markets do not take into account these kinds of costs, they are only partially efficient at allocating resources. Government plays an important role in remedying the deficiencies of markets in allocating resources.

Students need to investigate how markets function and how different events cause prices and wages to rise or fall. They need to study which costs and benefits markets take into account and which they fail to acknowledge. Markets are central to how incentives work in complex systems, so a thorough understanding of market function is central to making wise policy decisions.

Incentives

As I pointed out in Chapter 1, Great Britain solved the problem of prisoners dying on the trip to Australia by paying the ship captains based on the number of prisoners who arrived in good health rather than the number who set sail. Economists understand system behavior in terms of the incentives that operate in different situations. When there are social problems, economists would have us ask: How can we change the incentives so that we get the desired outcomes? We can illustrate this approach to problem solving with a couple of examples.

One area where incentives have clearly gone wrong in recent decades is the rising costs of health care. In part, this has occurred because health providers are paid for the procedures they carry out, such as transplants and MRI scans. This encourages them to conduct as many procedures as possible, especially expensive ones that provide greater reimbursement. To remedy this problem, society will have to find a way to pay health providers on the basis of how much their patients' health improves over time. Such an incentive system would encourage health providers to engage in preventive care, such as avoiding obesity, and to minimize the use of unnecessary expensive procedures.

If we are concerned about the fact that schools and community colleges do not prepare students for work, then we might consider changing the basis on which schools are funded. If schools are rewarded for the proportion of their students placed in appropriate jobs and the proportion of students who succeed in those jobs, then schools would have an incentive to make sure their students stay in school, learn useful skills, and understand what employers expect of them. Furthermore, schools would want to establish relationships with employers to place their students and make sure their students fulfill the needs of those employers. Currently, most schools make only limited efforts to help students make the transition to viable careers.

These examples illustrate the kinds of thinking required if society hopes to get incentives right. We need to teach students to think like economists when addressing problems. Students need to examine major societal problems and develop solutions that consider how the incentive structure might be changed to improve outcomes. Unfortunately, most politicians and voters have not been trained to think that way. If students develop their own proposed solutions to problems by using incentives, they will learn to think that way.

Globalization

Since World War II, there has been a steady growth in the globalization of the world economy, led by the rise of corporations that do business all over the world, such as Apple or Ford. These companies often move jobs to places that have lower wages, such as China and Mexico. This is having a profound effect on how economies in different countries function and is gradually spreading wealth to the far corners of the globe.

The globalized world creates new kinds of instability. Students should investigate how globalization is affecting prices and wages, the movement of jobs around the world, and how different countries are dealing with problems caused by globalization. These issues are causing great disruption to people's lives, as well as instability in the developed world, so students need to investigate strategies for dealing with the problems of globalization in their own countries. By trying to address real-world problems, students will begin to understand the complexity of the systems society must manage.

The Growth Rate of Countries

Students should study economic growth since the onset of the Industrial Revolution in order to understand the important factors that affect the success of different economies. Up until the Industrial Revolution, the growth rate of economies was negligible. Warfare was common, and it tended to undo whatever growth existed.

The Industrial Revolution in Great Britain saw a flowering of technological invention, producing many power tools such as the steam engine and the train. This led Great Britain to an average growth rate of 1% each year since about 1800. Starting in the 1800s, the United States began to learn the secrets of Great Britain's technological progress. In 1810, on a visit to Great Britain, American businessman Francis Cabot Lowell memorized the workings of British power looms. He took this knowledge back home and built the first textile mill in America.

But textile mills are not all that Americans stole from Britain. They also stole the idea of innovation itself. America produced many innovators, such as Thomas Edison and Henry Ford. Edison set up an invention laboratory in New Jersey, the first industrial research laboratory in the world. Given America's abundant natural resources, its growing population of immigrants, the people's entrepreneurial spirit, and their technological innovation, America managed an average growth rate of about 2% from the 1860s onward. America's great wealth was built on this growth over a period of 150 years. Of course, the fact that the country came out of two world wars mostly unscathed also helped immensely.

After World War II, the United States developed a number of institutions that further supported the country's economic growth. The federal government set up agencies to support research and development in universities and national laboratories. This led to the growth of large research universities, where researchers and their graduate students were funded to conduct research that led to new products and services. Many of these universities produced entrepreneurs who started businesses of their own. For example, Stanford University spawned Silicon Valley and the Massachusetts Institute of Technology (MIT) spawned many Boston area companies. Venture capital firms sprang up in these areas to fund the startup companies these universities produced. Research universities also attracted many bright foreign students to America. In fact, immigrants have been instrumental in creating many of the firms in Silicon Valley (Saxenian, 1999).

In the late 1940s, Japan adopted many American manufacturing techniques to grow the Japanese economy. From the early 1950s to 1990, Japan had an average growth rate of 7% a year. This high growth rate was made possible by the fact that the country invested a high percentage of its earnings in developing new plants, equipment, and products, and by the fact that they were playing "catch-up." That is, they were producing products that were first developed elsewhere, but that they could produce more cheaply with their low wages. Japanese growth slowed considerably after 1990, because the country had "caught up" and become a developed country.

Several Asian countries, such as Taiwan and South Korea and more recently China, adopted the Japanese model for growth. Between 1980 and 2010, China achieved an incredibly high growth rate of about 10% a year, dwarfing the average U.S. growth rate of about 2–3% a year. By one measure, China recently passed the United States in total production (labeled gross domestic product, or GDP). But China's population is four times larger than that of the United States, so China's people are only one-fourth as wealthy as Americans.

Since 2000, many countries in the developing world have had high growth rates, in the range of 5–7% a year, even in Africa. India has been growing at about that rate since the early 1990s. It seems that Japan provided a robust model that much of the world has copied. To sustain those high rates requires well-functioning governments that focus on growth and avoid warfare.

In summary, students should learn that there are many factors that affect the economic growth of countries. The most critical factors identified in this brief overview are invention and innovation; investment spending particularly for research, development, and education; good government, with a focus on growing the economy; avoidance of warfare; and an entrepreneurial spirit and financial support for innovation. Students should investigate the factors that affect the growth rate of countries and project trends in growth for different countries around the world. They can then examine how these trends will affect wealth and power in coming years.

TOWARD AN EDUCATION FOR CITIZENS OF A GLOBAL WORLD

Schools focus on the "hard" sciences of physics, chemistry, biology, and Earth science, even though most students will not pursue careers in science and the content of what is taught does not relate to their lives. I would argue that this emphasis is largely misplaced, because most of what students learn in these school subjects is not very helpful for making wise policy or personal decisions. These topics are important if you want to pursue a career in one of these sciences, but not for most people, who forget most of what they learn in their science classrooms.

In this chapter, I have emphasized economics, environmental science, and systems thinking. Chapter 3 emphasized medical science, and in Chapter

6, I'll stress understanding the foundations of mathematical and scientific thinking. These topics are much more relevant to most people's lives. They involve a mix of physical science, biological science, and social science. High schools in America and elsewhere treat them very lightly, though environmental science is beginning to establish a foothold in the curriculum.

To engage students in learning science, the projects and issues they work on should address serious issues in society. This not only makes learning science more engaging, but it also makes clear to students why it is important to study science. Many different societal issues require scientific understanding, such as how to feed a growing population and how to reduce the cost of treating the diseases of an overweight population. That's why these are the kinds of issues students should be tackling in school.

CHAPTER 6

Mathematical and Scientific Foundations

In his book *Introduction to Mathematical Thinking*, Keith Devlin (2012) argues: "Over many years, we have grown accustomed to the fact that advancement in an industrial society requires a workforce that has mathematical skills. But if you look more closely, those skills fall into two categories. The first category comprises people who, given a mathematical problem, can find its mathematical solution. The second category comprises people who can take a new problem, say in manufacturing, identify and describe key features of the problem mathematically, and use that mathematical description to analyze the problem in a precise fashion. In the past, there was a huge demand for employees with Type 1 skills, and a small need for people with Type 2 skills. . . . But in today's world, where companies must constantly innovate to stay in business, the demand is shifting toward Type 2 mathematical thinkers—to people who can think outside the mathematical box, not inside it" (p. 8).

As Devlin makes clear, mathematical thinking is more important than ever, and yet the mathematics curriculum still emphasizes solving well-defined problems using algorithms that can all be carried out by today's technology. Given the need for people with what Devlin calls Type 2 skills, students' time would be better spent learning how to use mathematical tools to define and solve real-world problems, rather than learning how to mimic algorithms that computers can perform faster and more efficiently than humans can. In fact, understanding how to apply computer tools appropriately requires much more thinking than executing algorithms. Learning Type 2 skills should become the new agenda for teaching mathematics.

In his book *The Global Achievement Gap*, Tony Wagner (2008) questions much of what we include in the mathematics curriculum in school. In particular, he asks why there is so much emphasis on algebra when most people never use it after they leave school. He points out: "Graduates from the Massachusetts Institute of Technology were recently surveyed regarding the math that this technically trained group used most frequently in their work. The assumption was that if any adults used higher-level math, it would be MIT grads. And while a few did, the overwhelming majority reported using nothing more than arithmetic, statistics, and probability" (p. 92). I would argue that it is likely they also use their basic understanding about different kinds of functions. In studying scientists, I find them talking about linear functions, exponential functions, growth functions, and asymptotic functions, as well as the distributions that pervade statistical thinking (Collins, 2011).

Ideally, students would learn in school how to *mathematize* the situations they find in the world. In order to mathematize a situation, it is necessary to formulate a question, decide what to measure, and then decide how to represent the data collected. For instance, a student might wonder where all her time goes and whether she could spend it more wisely. She might choose to keep a log of how much time she spends on each type of activity and decide she is spending too much time playing video games. She then might set a timer when she starts playing to remind her to stop at a fixed time. This is just one example of an infinite number of different situations that people can analyze mathematically.

RETHINKING THE MATH AND SCIENCE CURRICULUM

The foundations of mathematics and science are critical to everything we do in a complex society. In recent years, governments around the world have invested extensive resources in preparing students for careers in science, technology, engineering, and math (the so-called STEM disciplines), because governments now see these fields as vital to the future prosperity of their countries. The STEM disciplines are the basis for most of the inventions and innovations that support a growing economy. They are the disciplines that inform people in making decisions about complex issues. In simpler times, before the Industrial Revolution, people did not need a deep understanding of mathematics and science to make wise personal and public decisions, but as the technical complexity of the world has increased, these decisions have grown ever more difficult.

The easy availability of knowledge on the Internet has profoundly changed what is important to learn about science. In the past, people had to memorize a lot of information in order to make competent decisions, as doctors must do to make accurate diagnoses. But with easy access to knowledge, people can rely more on external memories to help them out. This is how doctors are using IBM's Watson for medical diagnosis. The essential skill is no longer memorization, but knowing how to reason scientifically, carry out investigations to answer important questions, and analyze the data collected. That is to say, students need to develop new learning skills rather than acquiring more information.

Computers also give us new ways to model and represent knowledge about the world. The challenge for schools is to change the emphasis from memorizing scientific facts to an emphasis on investigating meaningful issues and problems mathematically and scientifically. Below, I discuss critical ideas in math and science that should be the new focus of STEM education.

To learn how to mathematize situations and think scientifically, students need to investigate real problems in the world. In previous chapters, I've raised a number of issues that students can investigate mathematically and scientifically. For example, students can investigate how stock prices and price-earnings ratios vary over time. Similarly, they can study how world population, carbon dioxide levels, and habitat destruction vary over time and whether they are correlated. In the area of health, they can study the major causes of death at different ages and ways to prevent deaths from various causes. By carrying out their own investigations, students will learn much more deeply about the issues society faces in the 21st century.

WHAT STUDENTS SHOULD LEARN
ABOUT MATHEMATICAL FOUNDATIONS

The key ideas in mathematics get lost in the curriculum's emphasis on learning algorithms and solving well-defined problems. Here, I outline some of the ideas I think are central to a mathematical thinking in the modern world.

Variables

In algebra, x and y are used to represent variables, but scientists think about variables in a much richer way. They view variables as quantities or qualities that vary systematically. Perhaps the most common misconception about variables is that they have to be numeric. When *Consumer Reports* evaluates cars, it looks at many different variables—some of which are numeric, but many of which are not. For example, judgments about a car's ride and handling are essentially qualitative variables. You can turn these qualitative judgments into numeric variables by asking a sample of drivers to rate the ride and the handling on a scale, such as 1 to 10. But in doing this, much of the information about the quality of the ride and handling is lost, just as information about the quality of movies is lost in simply assigning some number of stars.

Students should learn about differences among the three common measures of central tendency for numeric variables: the *mean* (or average), *median*, and *mode*. Consider the salaries at Digiflop Corporation. Because executives earn huge salaries, their salaries pull up the average, which makes the mean not very representative of what most workers earn. The median salary is a much better measure when there is a skewed distribution, such as corporate salaries. The modal salary is likely to be even lower than the median, because corporations usually have a lot of workers who earn around the minimum wage.

Students need to address issues that involve using variables and measures of central tendency. For example, they might carry out consumer analyses of different products and activities, such as educational games or summer jobs, considering different qualities on which the products or activities vary and using mathematical tools for evaluating the products and activities. This will help them learn to mathematize their analyses of the phenomena they encounter in the world.

Graphs

Graphing is central to mathematizing and representing problems. Graphing allowed Galileo to see the systematic relation between the distance a body falls and the change in its velocity. Producing and interpreting graphs is difficult to learn and yet important to making sense of much of the discourse in a highly technological society about scientific and public policy issues.

Students should learn about at least four kinds of graphs that are commonly used to represent data: *line graphs*, *bar graphs*, *pie charts*, and *scatter plots*. Line graphs are particularly good for plotting trends and cycles in time-series data. They depend upon having continuous scales on both axes. Bar graphs are effective for displaying quantities over a discontinuous set of categories. For example, one can plot plant heights with a separate bar for each plant. Pie charts are used to show the relative size of the different parts of a whole. Scatter plots are very useful for investigating how two continuous variables interact with each other. They are a very good starting place to discover patterns between variables, and are an important tool for scientific inquiry.

As students mathematize different phenomena in the world, they should be doing a lot of graphing. For example, they can graph population, birth rates, and crime rates in different countries; long-term trends in GDP, stock market indexes, and the spread of democracy around the world; changes in sea level over millennia; and rates of heart disease and cancer in different countries. They can use scatter plots to look at correlations between variables such as age and heart attacks, gun ownership and homicides, education levels and growth rates, and other variables that have implications for personal and societal decisions. It would also be very useful for students to learn to use graphing programs, such as TinkerPlots, to construct dynamic visualizations of different phenomena of interest to them (Lehrer & Schauble, 2006).

Functions

A central concern in science is how to predict what will happen in the future. To do this, we have developed *formulas* that allow us to compute what will happen in different situations. Well-known examples of such formulas are $D = rt$ and $a = F/m$ (or $F = ma$). The first states that distance traveled is a direct function of the rate times the time traveled. The second formula, Newton's second law of motion, states that the acceleration of an object is a direct function of the force applied and an inverse function of the mass (or weight) of the object. Spreadsheets are a way to represent formulas on a computer and easily calculate the output for different input values.

Students should learn that a function is any formula that takes a set of inputs to produce an output. Input variables are called *independent variables* and output variables are called *dependent variables*. Many common functions take just one input variable that can be easily represented on a two-dimensional graph. For example, a *linear function* ($y = mx + b$) forms a straight line on the graph, where m is the *slope* of the line and b is the *y-intercept* (i.e. the value of x where the line crosses the y-axis). If Chris has a bank account with $20 and she decides to add $5 a month, her bank account (BA) will grow according to the function BA= $5n + 20$, where n is the number of months she contributes. Linear functions are a pervasive part of life.

A very important function for students to understand is the *exponential*. Exponential growth characterizes many kinds of situations, such as interest-bearing assets and the growth of a country's GDP. An exponential function represents a constant percentage growth rate. Money put into an interest-bearing asset grows slowly at first, but as interest accumulates and the value of the asset grows, it grows faster and faster. This is why it is important for students to save money when they are young, so they can reap the benefits of exponential growth of their savings.

If students study the growth of plants or the spread of new products in society, they will encounter the normal growth function. Many natural growth processes follow an S-shaped curve, such as the growth of flowers. Growth starts out slowly, speeds up exponentially, and then slows down as an *asymptote* is reached. Asymptotic functions are common in representing many natural phenomena. They occur whenever there is a ceiling or floor effect that limits further growth or decline.

One other function that students are likely to encounter is the *sine function*, which forms a uniform wave. Pure musical tones form *sine waves* that vary in frequency or cycles per second called Hertz, depending on the pitch of the note. Higher notes have higher frequencies. Overtones are high-frequency sine waves that accompany most notes when they are played on a musical instrument.

Students should study phenomena in the world that take the form of linear, exponential, sine, and normal growth functions. They should plot the graphs for these phenomena and make projections based on the curves plotted. These are some of the most important functions scientists and mathematicians use to describe phenomena, and students need to understand how they are used.

Statistics

In order to graph different phenomena and run statistical tests, students need to learn about distributions. When there is a distribution of values for a particular variable, such as students' grades on a test, the values are likely to fall on a normal curve (see Figure 6.1). Some normal distributions do not vary much, such as grades on an easy test, whereas others, such as grades on a difficult test, are likely to be much more variable. Hence, the curve for a difficult test would be more spread out than for the easy test. The degree to which the distribution is spread out around the mean μ of the distribution is described by the standard deviation σ.

As is clear from Figure 6.1, in a normal distribution, over 68% of the distribution lies within one standard deviation of the mean, over 95% within two standard deviations, and over 99% within three standard deviations (or three sigma). In manufacturing processes, companies often strive to produce defects at a rate less than six sigma. A six sigma process is one in which 99.9999998% of the products manufactured are statistically expected to be free of defects.

Students are likely to encounter other distributions as well. A *uniform distribution* occurs when you roll a die, where any number between one and six is equally likely to come up. A common distribution, the *binomial*, represents the number of heads or tails that occur if you flip a coin repeatedly for a fixed number of times. The shape of this kind of distribution is similar to a normal curve. A *Poisson distribution* expresses the probability of a given number of events occurring within a fixed interval of time, such as pieces of mail arriving each day. The larger the average number expected, the more it looks like a normal distribution.

Another common distribution is a *power law*, which describes the way many different phenomena are distributed in the world, such as the size of

Figure 6.1. Normal Distribution of Values

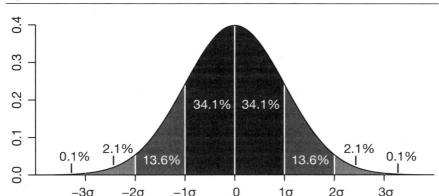

Adapted from a figure by M. W. Toews (https://commons.wikimedia.org/wiki/
File:Standard_deviation_diagram.svg). Licensed under Creative Commons.

municipalities and the frequency of words. A few municipalities are quite
large, while most are smaller. A few words are very frequent, but most are
infrequent. For example, in English the most common word, *the*, occurs
twice as often as the second most common word, *of*, and three times as often as the next most common word, *and*. A power law distribution follows
an 80-20 rule, where 20% of the cities have 80% of the population. Most
instances (e.g., municipalities or words) fall in the "long tail" that extends
to the right of the distribution. For such a distribution, the median is much
more representative of municipality size or word frequency than the mean,
which is skewed by the few cases of cities of large size and words of high frequency. Students need to understand that not all distributions are normal,
and how to work with other distributions.

Statistical analysis pervades the way companies and scientists analyze
data. Students need to understand enough statistics to run statistical tests
on experiments they conduct and evaluate claims they encounter in public
discourse. Students should also plot a variety of distributions of phenomena
to get a sense of what kinds of phenomena follow which distribution patterns. Below, I discuss how scientists analyze data from experiments in order
to derive conclusions about the world.

Correlation

Because many arguments are based on correlations, it is important for students to understand the power and limitations of correlational data. When
two variables are correlated, they are often causally linked in some way, but

not always. There is a famous example of hormone replacement therapy (HRT) for women, which was found to correlate with a lower probability of getting heart disease. This led doctors to recommend HRT to older women for many years. But randomized trials, where HRT was given to half the subjects and a placebo to the other half, showed that HRT actually significantly *increased* the probability of heart disease. Such randomized trials are the gold standard for determining causality. Studies investigating the discrepancy in the two results showed that the women who received HRT previously had come from a wealthier population, and were more likely to engage in healthy eating and exercise, which lowered their chance of getting heart disease. So the correlation of lower rates of heart disease with HRT was based on a biased sample of women. Misinterpretation of correlation data is common, and students should learn to ask if there are other factors that might cause a spurious relationship.

Even when a causal relation exists between two variables, it is not clear which way the causality runs. For example, suppose there is a correlation between how happy children rate themselves and how well they do in school. Perhaps happy children do not worry about much and so they are able to concentrate on their schoolwork, or maybe children who do well in school get psychic rewards that make them happy. Both scenarios are possible, and the two variables may, in fact, influence each other. Or it may be that another factor, such as parental wealth, influences both how happy children are and how well they do in school. We simply cannot tell from correlation data how causality is involved in such a case.

Students should analyze and plot correlations between different variables they are interested in to learn how correlations vary and the strengths and limitations of correlational evidence. They should make scatter plots of correlational data, plot regression lines, and compute the correlations mathematically. Many policy arguments in the public domain are based on correlational evidence, and students need to be able to evaluate such arguments to make wise decisions.

Making Inferences from Statistics

Because all measurement involves error, students need to learn how to estimate confidence in the results of their experiments. They also need to understand how scientists analyze experiments to reach their conclusions, such as whether a particular drug is effective. Suppose a neuroscientist gives a drug that is thought to improve memory to a random sample of 100 subjects and a placebo to another 100 subjects. A memory test might then be given to see how many items each subject can recall. Let's say the group given the drug can recall 25.7 items on average out of 40 items, while the placebo group can only recall an average of 22.4 items. Although the averages for the two groups are different, there is an overlap between the test scores for different subjects. The measurement question, then, is whether the difference is accidental or a result of the effects of the drug. Scientists have developed statistical tests to decide such questions. Students can use computer programs to carry out statistical tests by entering the conditions of the experiment and the data collected.

Sometimes two or more variables are manipulated in a particular experiment. Such an experiment calls for an *analysis of variance*. Suppose in the drug experiment described above, we treated males and females separately to see whether the drug had the same effects for both genders. We might also look at the effects of the drug at three different ages—say, 15, 25, and 35. Both age and gender would be *between-subjects variables* because we would need different groups of subjects for each condition. We might also decide to make the drug versus placebo conditions a *within-subjects variable* by testing the same subjects under both conditions on different days. We can counterbalance any order effects by giving half the subjects the placebo first and the other half the drug first. We also may want to control for other variables, such as income, to guard against spurious results. In this study, age, gender, and drug versus placebo are the independent variables, and scores on the memory test are the dependent variable.

We can represent hypothetical results of the experiment by showing the average improvement in recalled items for the different groups of subjects from the placebo to the drug condition, as shown in Table 6.1.

These hypothetical results suggest that the effect of the drug seems positive overall, seems to increase with age, and may be stronger for women than men. There also is a possible interaction between age and gender, where women show a larger increase in the effect of the drug with age and men less so. The question is whether these effects are statistically significant and how big the effects are. To find out, one can use an analysis-of-variance program by specifying the conditions used in the experiment and entering the data for each subject.

Students should conduct experiments on phenomena they care about. For example, Barbara White had middle school students conduct an

Table 6.1. Mean Improvements Using the Drug

	Age			
	15	25	35	Mean
Males	2.0	2.1	2.2	2.1
Females	1.8	2.3	2.5	2.2
Mean	1.9	2.2	2.35	2.15

experiment on how music affected students' ability to do math problems. A class tested itself on different days working comparable sets of math problems in a fixed period of time with or without music playing. The results showed that they did worse on the problems with the music than without, much to the students' consternation. They ran statistical tests on their results to determine whether the difference was significant. In this experiment, they learned how statistics can be used to understand phenomena better.

When students learn to mathematize the world, they often find surprising patterns in the data. These patterns then lead to further inquiry to uncover the underlying reasons for the patterns. This is an essential aspect of scientific inquiry and discovery. It is the process that Keith Devlin ascribes to Type 2 individuals, who look for patterns in the world that they can make sense of, rather than simply doing the routine work of their jobs. Often, these people can find better ways to do their work or ingenious solutions to problems. It is their kind of curiosity that made the Industrial Revolution possible and will make future innovations possible.

WHAT STUDENTS SHOULD LEARN ABOUT SCIENTIFIC FOUNDATIONS

Students need to learn about the fundamentals of the scientific process to analyze issues and make sense of the arguments that pervade government policy. Science is an iterative process by which society slowly converges on an understanding of how the world works. To explain different phenomena, scientists create theories and models, which they justify with appeals to logic and evidence. Other scientists often try to refute those claims with competing theories and evidence. This process of claims and counterclaims goes on until a consensus is reached as to which theory best reflects all the evidence collected to date. Sometimes, that consensus is later overthrown when new evidence comes to light that undermines the previous consensus, as when Einstein's theory of relativity amended the Newtonian consensus about time and motion.

Students should learn to view scientific inquiry as a process of oscillating between theory and evidence, where researchers develop and test alternative scientific models and theories. The ultimate goal is to create a model and develop arguments to support that model, and thereby convince other researchers of the model's merits. This view of scientific inquiry reflects the way most sciences include two camps: the theoreticians and the empiricists. Theory and empirical investigation form the two poles of science. Research questions form a bridge between these two poles, in which competing theories generate alternative hypotheses about the answer to a research question, which then are tested through empirical investigation. Analysis and synthesis form the other bridge between the poles by providing ways to represent and interpret data from an investigation so that the data bear on the theories in competition and synthesize a new "best theory."

This inquiry cycle of science is embedded in the standard form of research articles—that is, with sections for an introduction, methods, results, and discussion. The introduction relates the investigation to existing theory and derives the research questions and hypotheses that the investigation addresses. The methods section describes how the investigation was carried out. The results section describes the data analyses and the findings. The discussion section then brings the analyses back to existing theory and how it should be modified based on the findings. Hence, the inquiry cycle is deeply embedded in the culture of science.

In the next four sections, I describe scientific knowledge in terms of its four components: (1) theories and models, (2) forming research questions and hypotheses, (3) designing and carrying out investigations, and (4) data analysis and synthesis. Students need to understand these different components as they carry out investigations in different areas.

Theories and Models

Scientific models are representations that scientists create to capture specific aspects of phenomena in the world. Recurring patterns or forms are found among different scientific models (Collins & Ferguson, 1993; White, Collins, & Frederiksen, 2011). Some of the different forms models take include constraint equations, stage models, hierarchies, and system dynamics models. Students should learn how to carry out investigations of phenomena guided by these target structures, which I refer to as *model types*, as well as the processes that guide model construction, which I call *modeling strategies*.

In school, students often engage in the most basic modeling strategies, such as determining the stages in a process or analyzing trends. Any inquiry can be pursued more or less systematically. For example, if students are comparing two phenomena, one simple way of doing this is to list the characteristics of each. This is the simplest compare-and-contrast strategy. The two resulting lists may shed light on how the two phenomena are alike and different. A more constrained form of this strategy involves choosing a set of dimensions that apply to both phenomena being compared, and then filling in the value on each of these dimensions for both phenomena (for an example of dimensions and values, see the description of stage models below).

In the following sections, I describe three different model types: (1) *structural models* for analyzing the structure of phenomena, (2) *causal and functional models* for analyzing causal or functional aspects of phenomena, and (3) *behavioral models* for describing the dynamic behavior of phenomena. Students need to learn about the most common model types in order to analyze the kinds of issues discussed in previous chapters.

Structural models. The simplest and most common models describe the structure of a system. Among the structural models, *spatial decomposition* is the kind of analysis that takes place in anatomy or circuit diagrams. The goal is to break an entity down into a set of nonoverlapping parts and specify the relationships among the parts. The set of constraints includes coverage of the entire entity, specifying the connections, and, where applicable, specifying the nature of the connection. Connections are sometimes simply points of contact, as in a circuit, or they may be more complex, as in anatomy. Students might construct a structural model of the different systems in the body and how they interconnect.

Temporal decompositions or *stage models* are common in historical analysis, psychological analysis, and the analysis of any process characterized by qualitative states. The simplest stage model is a list constructed with the constraint that the stages follow one another sequentially without overlap. In a more complicated version of stage models, shown in Figure 6.2, each stage might be characterized by multiple characteristics (Char.), and furthermore, these characteristics may be arranged on a set of dimensions (Dim.). As a simple example, a first stage might show that a boy was angry and tired before his nap, and happy and energetic afterward. The interrelationship among the variables might be specified (for example, energy determines mood), and the reason for the change from one stage to the next specified (for instance, a nap leads to increased energy). These last four constraints (multiple characteristics, specified dimensions, specified interrelationships, and reasons for transition) are all optional constraints that a

Figure 6.2. Stage Models

	Stage 1	Stage 2	Stage 3	Stage 4
	Char. on Dim 1	Char. on Dim 1	Char. on Dim 1	Char. on Dim 1
	Char. on Dim 2	Char. on Dim 2	Char. on Dim 2	Char. on Dim 2
	Char. on Dim 3	Char. on Dim 3	Char. on Dim 3	Char. on Dim 3
	Char. on Dim n	Char. on Dim n	Char. on Dim n	Char. on Dim n

Interrelationships (left axis) → Timeline (right)

Reasons for Transition   Reasons for Transition   Reasons for Transition

Source: Collins & Ferguson (1993).

person might or might not use in constructing a stage model. Students might construct a stage model of human life, much as Shakespeare did with the seven stages of life speech in *As You Like It*.

Cost-benefit analysis is a special case of compare and contrast used in social and economic policy analysis. The things compared in cost-benefit analysis are alternative courses of action, which requires one to first identify all possible courses of action (the coverage constraint), then to try to identify all the costs and benefits (or pros and cons) of each alternative. This might also involve a set of dimensions on which the alternatives are compared, such as time, effort, and money. To be thorough, it is important to look for possible side effects, for social as well as individual effects, and for possible countereffects and synergies. High school students might do a cost-benefit analysis of owning a car or going to college near their home.

The search for primitive elements has driven much of the history of the physical sciences. The ancient Greeks had the view that everything was made of four elements: earth, air, fire, and water. Chemistry later came up with 92 natural elements, and when atoms were discovered, the quest was to determine the basic elements from which atoms are made, such as electrons, protons, and neutrons. The goal is to characterize a large set of phenomena (such as substances or actions) as made up of combinations of a small number of primitive elements (see Figure 6.3). Coverage of all the phenomena by the set of primitive elements is particularly critical in this effort. Another constraint is to specify how the elements combine to produce each phenomenon. Students might try to construct a primitive elements model of human emotions.

Tree-structure or *hierarchy analysis* is familiar to everyone. It is used for many kinds of analysis, such as categorizing plants and animals. The constraint in a hierarchy is that the elements must be broken into subsets of similar types (the similarity constraint). These kinds of hierarchies

Figure 6.3. Primitive Elements

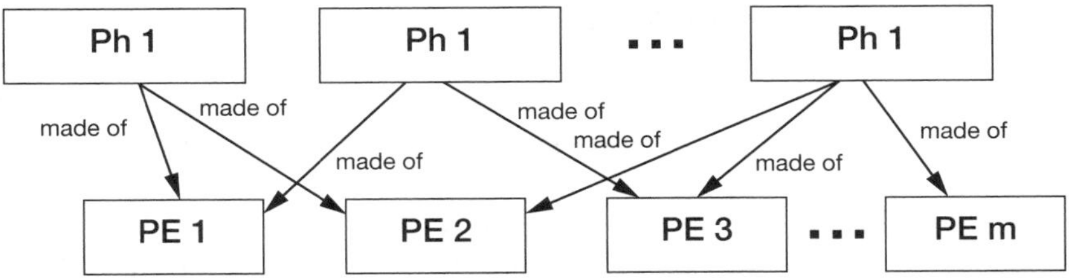

Ph=phenomenon
PE=Primitive Element, m<<n

Source: Collins & Ferguson (1993).

pervade the biological and social sciences, because evolutionary processes naturally produce tree structures. Hence, people are prone to look for them everywhere.

A more constrained form of analysis is *cross-product analysis*. The best-known example is the Periodic Table of chemical elements. Construction of the table led to identifying missing elements and ultimately to an understanding of the atomic structure of molecules. But it is possible to attempt to decompose any set of elements into an array characterized by a set of dimensions. For example, students could array vehicles by their medium (air, land, ice, and so forth) and their form of propulsion (motor, sail, and so on). The dimensions can be continuous or discrete, and slots in the table can be multiply filled or not. But, as with primitive elements, coverage of all the cases is a critical constraint in cross-product analysis.

Students might analyze different issues using structural models. For example, they could use cost-benefit analysis to analyze different sources of energy. They could use hierarchical analysis to analyze different species of dinosaurs or types of governments. They could construct a stage model of how human society has evolved. Students can analyze any number of questions of interest and importance using structural analyses.

Causal and functional models. To analyze why phenomena occur, students should learn to construct causal and functional models. Among the causal models, *critical-event analysis* occurs in historical analysis and trouble-shooting of various kinds (when diagnosing the causes of crashes and explosions, it is called *critical-incident analysis*). This kind of analysis centers on a particular event (such as an airplane crash or the invention of the printing press). It attempts to identify the events or causes that led to the critical event or the set of consequences that flow from the critical event. High school students might analyze traffic accidents to identify the different causes of each.

Causal chain analysis is a variation on critical-event analysis that assumes a sequence of events, each one leading to the next. It is frequently used in constructing sequential models of events. For example, an earthquake caused a bridge to vibrate, which led a defective steel girder to fall, causing a gap that cars fell into. The analysis distinguishes triggering events or causes from preconditions (for instance, defective steel) necessary for the triggering event to cause the effects. Each effect, in turn, can be the triggering event for a new set of effects. This analysis breaks the continuous stream of events in the world into a train of events that are causally interlinked. The chain of events leading to World War I would be an interesting model for students to construct.

Problem-centered analysis is found throughout history and in any subject area where human goals and actions are paramount. The simplest form of this analysis breaks an event stream into problems and the actions taken to solve the problems. These actions lead to main effects and side effects. Side effects often represent new problems to be solved. As a philosopher once said, "The chief cause of problems is solutions."

Multifactor analysis is another common way to analyze causality in systems. It is particularly pervasive in psychology and medicine, but it is also common in many other disciplines where it is difficult to identify a chain of causally interlinked events. In multifactor theories, variables (called factors or independent variables) are linked together in a tree structure. The branches of the tree are linked together using the word *and* (ANDed) if a set of factors are all necessary to produce the desired value on the dependent variable. They are linked together with the word *or* (ORed) if any of the factors are sufficient to produce the desired value on the dependent variable. A multifactor analysis constructed by one of my former students is shown in Figure 6.4.

Form and function analysis involves different structures depending on the field of inquiry, such as mechanics or biology. One can analyze the workings of physical devices, such as a car engine, in terms of functions, structures, and mechanisms. The function is the goal that the device (for example, a piston) accomplishes; the structure is made up of components of the device that accomplish the function; and the mechanism is the process

Figure 6.4. A Student's Analysis of the Causal Factors Affecting Rice Growing

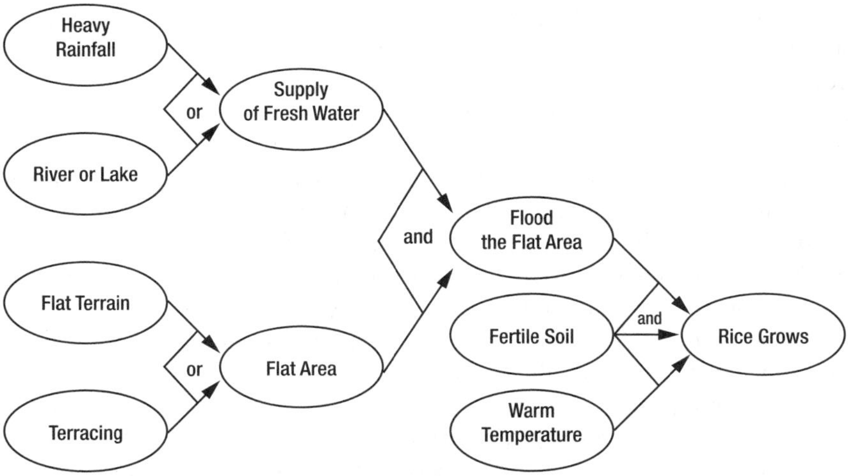

Source: Collins & Ferguson (1993).

by which the structure accomplishes the function. In biology, functions consist of abilities, such as flying or stalking, that enable animals to execute their behaviors, such as hunting. Features, such as wings, are the structural forms that enable animals to execute their functions. Mechanisms describe how features, such as wings, enable a bird to fly. It would be a good exercise for students to construct a form and function analysis of a biological or mechanical system. Form and function analysis is pervasive in describing complex systems.

Students should construct a variety of causal and functional models to enhance their understanding of model building and underlying causal processes. For example, they might construct a model of how greenhouse gases cause the Earth to warm, they might construct a model of how a rise in interest rates causes the economy to slow, or they might construct a model of how smoking causes lung cancer or heart disease. Constructing such models will help them deeply understand issues that will affect their lives.

Behavioral models. Among the behavioral models, system dynamics models are increasingly common, especially in the social and physical sciences. Computer programs that schools have used, such as Stella, provide tools for constructing system dynamics models (Mandinach & Cline, 2013). The basic elements in a system dynamics model are variables that can increase or decrease. These are linked together by positive or negative links, usually with feedback loops permeating the system of variables. These models can have lags built into the system. Students might construct a system dynamics model for any of the examples Donella Meadows (2008) described as system problems, recounted in Chapter 5.

Agent models are constructed frequently to explain behavior in the physical and biological sciences, particularly the behavior of small particles such as molecules and bacteria, or agents such as rabbits and humans. Various computer programs, such as NetLogo, are used to construct these models (Wilensky, 1999; Wilensky & Reisman, 2006; Wilensky & Resnick, 1999). These models assume parallel interaction of a large array of elements according to specified rules. When the elements encounter one another, a number of possible interactions occur under different conditions. For example, students have constructed agent models of predator-prey behavior and models of how contagion spreads in populations.

Constraint systems have permeated our understanding of physical systems since the time of Galileo. They are characterized by a set of equations describing the behavior of a system. Like system dynamics models, the elements in constraint systems are variables, but they are not simulation models like system dynamics models or agent models. To construct such a model, one tries to manipulate one variable while holding other variables constant to determine the effect of the first variable on the dependent variable, just as Galileo did. For example, Galileo was able to determine the acceleration attributable to gravity by rolling a ball down a sloping ramp for different distances. It might be a good exercise for students to construct a constraint equation to describe the behavior of gases based on conducting experiments, as in Boyle's law.

Situation-action models are commonly used to describe behavior in the social sciences. They are characterized by a set of rules of the form "If in situation x, do y." The situation can change either because the world changes or because the agent takes an action. Some of the most sophisticated models for simulating human behavior are situation-action models (Anderson, 1993; Newell & Simon, 1972). It would be good for students to construct a simulation-action model of interaction over the telephone where people respond in systematic ways to things that are said, based on simple rules.

Trend analysis is most commonly found in economics and history, but it can be used to analyze any set of variables that change over time. In economics, trend analysis often involves identifying *leading indicators*, or variables that tend to show variation patterns before the variables of most interest. For example, stock prices tend to rise or fall before similar changes in a country's production and income. It would be good for students to analyze economic trends to see if they can identify leading indicators for different variables.

An example of the trend analysis is shown in Figure 6.5. V1 shows increasing exponential growth, such as occurs for the gross national product (GNP) of a country. V2 shows a normal growth function, which starts slowly and speeds up till it reaches an asymptote, as characterized the growth of telephones in the United States. V3 and V4 show cyclical variables, such as the inflation rate and price/earnings ratio of stocks (P/E ratio). As shown, inflation rate is a leading indicator for the P/E ratio.

Students should construct behavioral models about phenomena that are of interest to them. For example, they might construct an agent model of predator-prey relationships, a trend analysis of GDP in different countries during the 20th century, or a system dynamics model of how climate works. Given the growing importance of modeling in science, students need to learn about the different forms models can take and how various models can be linked together to form a coherent theory.

Research Questions and Hypotheses

In order to evaluate models and theories, students need to learn how to formulate research questions that can be directly investigated. Sometimes, research questions are quite vague (such as, What are the precursors to heart disease?),

Figure 6.5. Trend Analysis

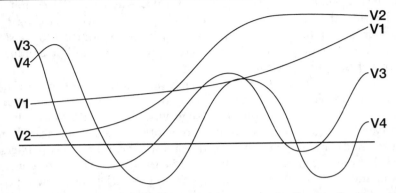

- Variable 1 is exponentially increasing (e.g., gross national product).
- Variable 2 is a standard growth function (e.g., the number of telephones).
- Variables 3 and 4 are cyclical variables (e.g., price-to-earnings [P/E] ratio), and 3 is a leading indicator for 4 (e.g., inflation rate for P/E ratio).

Source: Collins & Ferguson (1993).

and sometimes the questions are specific (for instance, Does taking a particular drug reduce cholesterol?). The hypotheses in any study are the different possible answers to a research question, which can be based on alternative theoretical positions. For example, the Framingham Heart Study, which started in 1948, tried to identify precursors to heart disease. Researchers identified more than 200 possible precursors to measure, and followed 5,000 people in Framingham, Massachusetts, over time to see if they developed heart disease. These 200 variables were the researchers' alternative hypotheses as to what might affect the chance of getting heart disease. The study identified smoking, blood pressure, and cholesterol levels, among other things, as contributing to the likelihood of getting heart disease.

Different types of models generate different types of research questions. Table 6.2 gives examples of the types of questions that arise in constructing structural, causal, and behavioral models. These are not an exhaustive set of questions needed to construct the different types of models, but they are some of the most common research questions that arise as scientists create models to express and develop their theoretical ideas.

Students should learn to frame research questions and hypotheses about important issues they can design experiments to test. For example, they could frame a question about whether students who eat more fruits and vegetables feel better than those who eat more sweets and starches. Hypotheses might be that students who eat fruits and vegetables gain less weight and have more energy. Another kind of question students might consider is the psychological effect of saving money over the course of a year. They might

Table 6.2. Types of Research Questions Generated by Different Model Types

Model Type	Examples of Questions
Structural	What are all the different types of X? What are the characteristics of X? What stages does X go through as it evolves? What are the components of X and how are they related?
Causal	Does Y cause X? What effect does Y have on X? What causes X to happen? What are all the factors that affect X?
Behavioral	How will X behave in the future? What conditions cause a move from state A to B? What are the rules of interaction between X and Y? What process produces X?

hypothesize that saving money will lead students to feel more secure and self-satisfied. Students might investigate a wide variety of topics that could deepen their understanding of important issues they will face in future.

Designing Investigations

There are many different investigation methods, but they generally fall into two basic types: (1) exploratory investigations and (2) confirmatory investigations. Exploratory investigations are employed when one has broad research questions and some general theoretical ideas, which suggest interesting data sources to study. The goal is to obtain data that will constrain efforts to develop more detailed models and theories. Confirmatory investigations, on the other hand, are used when one has a well-developed model or a set of competing models that allow one to make predictions. The goal is to test the hypotheses to see if the findings are consistent with the theoretical predictions. This determines which models are most consistent with the data.

Galileo is famous for developing exploratory methods in science. In his experiments on pendulums and gravity, he systematically varied the elements that he thought might affect the period of the pendulum and the speed of a ball rolling down an incline. From these exploratory investigations, he derived equations for the motion of pendulums and falling bodies. The Framingham Heart Study was exploratory, using natural variation rather than controlled manipulation.

The kind of data collected in exploratory investigations has a strong effect on the types of models that can be constructed. Quantitative data support the construction of constraint-equation models, as we see with Galileo, or multifactor models, as we see in the Framingham Heart Study. The goal of exploratory studies is to identify patterns in the data that allow for the construction of models. These models can then be evaluated using confirmatory methods. Confirmatory investigations, which are designed to test theory-based hypotheses, can take many different forms. The best known is the randomized trial, which I described above.

Students should conduct both exploratory and confirmatory investigations during their school years. For example, to test the question about eating fruits and vegetables versus junk foods, they could provide snacks of either kind to a group of students and then test the subjects 2 hours later as to how energetic and how hungry they feel using a five-point scale. Or they might run a long-term study in which they enlist a group of students to change their diet to eat a healthy one featuring fruits, vegetables, and nuts, compared to a control group that makes no dietary change. They might weigh the students and conduct a health survey before and after to see the effects of the change in diet. To investigate the effects of saving money, they might construct an attitude survey, which they administer before and after a long period during which students save different amounts of money. Having students learn to carry out investigations will better prepare them for a world where success in life depends on the ability to figure out how to make things work.

Data Analysis and Synthesis

Data analyses are systematic procedures for examining the information obtained in an investigation. Data analysis methods can be characterized as either qualitative or quantitative. Although the methods for analyzing qualitative versus quantitative data may differ, the primary goals of the analysis remain the same.

The main purpose of data analysis is to support the development of convincing arguments, which show how the findings from an investigation support particular conclusions and have implications for theories. Data analyses examine the information obtained in order to meet several objectives in developing and testing models and theories. These include the following:

1. *Creating representations that will reveal patterns:* One objective is to display data in ways that summarize the data and reveal patterns. Sometimes the same data can be displayed in multiple ways to reveal different patterns.

2. ***Interpreting how data provide evidence with respect to competing hypotheses:*** A second objective is to use patterns found in the data to determine which hypotheses are supported or refuted by the data.

3. ***Exploring the data to develop new models, theories, and ideas for further research:*** Another objective is to search the various representations of the data for unanticipated phenomena or relationships among variables. Discoveries made through this process may lead to modifying an existing model or to creating new models and theories.

4. ***Establishing the generality of the findings:*** A final purpose of data analyses is to provide evidence regarding the generality of a theoretical model—the range of circumstances to which it applies.

Students should develop representations of data from their own investigations and from the many data sets available online, addressing important issues that will affect their lives in future. In creating representations, older students should go beyond using static representations, such as bar charts and scatter plots, to create more dynamic representations using online graphing programs, such as TinkerPlots or NetLogo. They also should write up interpretations of the data, explaining how they relate to theories and models of the phenomena represented.

IMPLICATIONS FOR MATH AND SCIENCE EDUCATION

There is a growing demand for people who can use mathematics creatively and think scientifically, even if they are not scientists. Yet most of what passes for math and science education in school consists of learning to carry out fixed procedures and memorizing large numbers of facts and definitions that students soon forget. This is largely time wasted, when students could be taught to analyze different kinds of phenomena and situations that are central to issues in society using mathematical and scientific methods. This would prepare them much more effectively for the world they are entering and would be much more interesting and challenging.

The ability to systematically analyze situations, design new solutions, and test them out experimentally are critical skills in many different occupations, such as farming, consulting, management, and most technical professions. Students would do well to learn the way scientists approach problems for navigating through an increasingly complex world.

CHAPTER 7

Passion Schools
A New Vision for School and Curriculum

In *Rethinking Education in the Age of Technology*, Richard Halverson and I (Collins & Halverson, 2009) argue: "Though innovative teachers often find ways to embed learning in meaningful tasks, much of school is like learning tennis by being told the rules and practicing the forehand, backhand, and serve without ever playing or seeing a tennis match. Students are taught algebra and parsing of sentences without being given any idea of how algebra and parsing might be useful in their lives. That is not how a coach would teach you to play tennis. A coach might first show you how to grip and swing the racket, but very soon you would be hitting the ball and playing games. A good coach would have you go back and forth between playing games and working on particular skills. The essential idea in teaching skills is to tightly couple a focus on accomplishing real-world tasks with a focus on the underlying competencies needed to carry out the tasks" (p. 23).

This final chapter presents a vision for restructuring schooling to teach 21st-century skills and knowledge to 21st-century students. In such a school, students are placed in curricula based on their interests, rather than the grade they are in. Designed into each curriculum would be the kinds of skills, knowledge, and dispositions described in this book. Students would be encouraged to stick with a particular curriculum for a long time, perhaps several years, while they develop deep understanding.

Children might start off in the early years studying topics of particular interest, such as pets, families, vehicles, or dinosaurs. But as children advance, they would move into curricula that reflect the kinds of things adults do in the world, such as the arts, business, medicine, communications, teaching, law, or engineering. Each curriculum would include the foundational knowledge and skills I have outlined in the previous chapters. The plan would be for students to start out in two of these curricula, move on to other curricula as they progress, and specialize more as they move through high school. Over their years in school, they might engage in eight or ten different curricula. The assumption is that students can change from one curriculum to another, with the agreement of teachers and the students' parents. But they should not change curricula frequently or they will never develop deep skills and knowledge in any domain.

In summary, my vision, which I call a passion curriculum, incorporates important principles for the redesign of schooling, in order to make teaching and learning more appropriate for developing the skills and knowledge that will be needed in the 21st century. It embodies authentic tasks and assessments, a dual focus on the teaching of particular competencies in the context of accomplishing meaningful tasks, development of deep skills and knowledge, peer teaching and mentoring, and a learning cycle of planning, doing, and reflecting. The goal is to develop schooling that will have a major impact on student motivation and learning, and will better prepare students for the complex world they are entering.

ELEMENTS OF A NEW VISION FOR AMERICAN SCHOOLS

Around the country, some schools are instituting elements of this vision of how schools can address the kinds of knowledge and skills required for living in a complex society. But no schools I know of have put together all the elements needed to foster the kind of learning that will help students thrive in the 21st century.

New School Designs

Farsighted leaders have come up with new school designs that incorporate many of the elements I think are important in designing schools that will prepare students for productive careers in a complex society.

Central Park East Secondary School. In her book *The Power of Their Ideas*, Deborah Meier (1995) described her design for Central Park East Secondary School (CPESS) in Harlem, New York City, which Frederick Wiseman captured in his film *High School II* (Wiseman, 1994). Her design ideas have spread to other schools around the country, such as the high-tech schools in San Diego, California. The design incorporated several elements that I think are important. Meier's school, populated mostly by minority children, was unique in its emphasis on community service and the five Habits of Mind listed in Chapter 1. In the school's Senior Institute, students spent much of their last 2 years working on 14 challenges to put together a portfolio needed for graduation. A small committee made up of the student's advisor, other faculty, and other students evaluated each of the 14 portfolio challenges based on rubrics that were widely available to students in the school. The committee for each challenge was like a doctoral committee in a university.

The 14 challenges covered a wide range of knowledge and skills that the school regarded as important to become a lifelong learner and productive citizen (Darling-Hammond, Ancess, & Falk, 1995). The products students created for each challenge took many different forms, such as essays, videos, and performances. The 14 challenges included the following:

1. Developing a postgraduate plan for their life, which guides students' selection of projects for the other challenges
2. Producing an autobiographical work
3. Explaining what they learned from their community service
4. Developing a product (for example, a debate or op-ed piece) addressing an ethical or social issue
5. Producing an aesthetic expression, including both performance and critique
6. Demonstrating an understanding of mass media and their effects
7. Demonstrating an understanding of practical issues such as computers, health, legal issues, employment, and independent living
8. Demonstrating an ability to use geographical tools such as maps or a geographic information system (GIS)
9. Providing evidence for knowledge of a second language
10. Carrying out a scientific investigation and demonstrating knowledge of science
11. Carrying out a math investigation and demonstrating ability to solve math problems
12. Carrying out a historical investigation and demonstrating knowledge of history
13. Demonstrating understanding of literature in different genres
14. Demonstrating physical skills, such as participation in a sport

This portfolio covered a much wider conception of proficiency than do the standardized tests in American schools, and covered most of the proficiencies that standardized tests ignore, as listed in Chapter 1.

High Tech Schools (www.hightechhigh.org) form a network of K–12 charter schools with more than 5,000 students in the San Diego area. The schools are guided by four connected design principles—equity, personalization, authentic work, and collaborative design. They have a diverse student body and an emphasis on college entrance and completion for all. Students pursue their passions through projects, and reflect on their learning, with a focus on the five Habits of Mind developed at CPESS. Projects address a wide variety of topic areas across the arts and sciences, including health, economics, and the environment. Students connect their studies to the world through fieldwork, community service, internships, and consultation with outside experts. With students as design partners, staff members function as reflective practitioners, conducting inquiry into equitable teaching and learning, school culture, project design, and authentic assessment.

Summit Public Schools (summitps.org/student-day?day=1) are a high school charter school system. Summit Public Schools incorporate many features that can help prepare students for the 21st century. The schools emphasize work on real-world projects in different subject areas. Projects involve problem solving, creative and critical thinking, working with others, and communication skills. Students have a personalized learning plan that they work out with a mentor and they proceed at their own pace through their studies, with one-on-one tutoring and peer learning. The mentors counsel students on college and career goals, foster reflection on successes and challenges, and encourage self-directed learning to reach their goals. The students join community groups and are encouraged to participate in after-school sports and clubs. These different activities foster the knowledge and skills needed for a graduation portfolio similar to the CPESS portfolio described above.

AltSchools (https://www.altschool.com/), which were started by a Google executive interested in personalization, are developing private micro-schools at the elementary and middle school level around the country. They develop personalized learning plans for each student, which emphasize coverage across the curriculum and going deep into areas the student is passionate about. Students of different ages are mixed together and work to support one another. Over their 8 years in the school, they put together a digital portfolio of all the work they have done. The curriculum emphasizes inquiry projects, core skills, and reflection. Technology is pervasive throughout the school and central to much of the work students do. The school develops a sense of community, and students learn to value diversity, fairness, and compassion.

Community-of-Learners Model. Barbara Rogoff (1994) described an elementary school designed around a community-of-learners model, as opposed to the knowledge-transmission model that permeates most schools in America. Parents committed to spending 3 hours each week in the classroom working as teacher aides. Teachers worked with students to decide on projects to carry out and served as guides when the students encountered difficulties. Most of the day, students worked in small groups. Students chose the activities they would participate in from among some required activities and optional activities. The curriculum was built on children's curiosity about what is happening in the world. Students stayed with the same teacher for 2 years, and second-year students helped guide first-year students in their groups. There were no grades given. Instead, teachers and students regularly produced reports for parents describing what students had learned and the challenges they faced, which guided their future work.

In the school, which may have changed since Rogoff's (1994) description, students became self-directed learners, working with others to make decisions and help out when challenges arise. The children loved the school and helped parents, serving as aides, understand the goals of the current activities by providing background knowledge for what was happening. Children liked the authority this provided and the sense of accomplishment they felt when they completed a project. They often were sorry to go on vacation. The school embodied many of the features required to engage children in taking responsibility for their own education.

Curricular Innovations

Problem-Based Learning. Howard Barrows first developed problem-based learning (PBL) to teach medical students how doctors do diagnosis (Barrows & Tamblyn, 1980). It has since formed the basis for the curriculum in several medical schools and spread to a few engineering schools and high schools. The core of the method is to present ill-defined cases (for instance, a 65-year-old man complaining of stomach pains) to a group of medical students who have to ask questions and run tests in order to identify all the symptoms of the disease they are trying to diagnose. A facilitator provides the test results they request based on an actual case and guides the process of their investigation.

Students work on a whiteboard with information in four columns:

1. Facts of the case—symptoms identified
2. Ideas and hypotheses—possible diagnoses
3. Learning issues—what must be studied to narrow down the possible hypotheses
4. Action plan—what students will do to come up with a diagnosis

Students divide up the learning issues and go off on their own to study each one. They come back later to exchange the information they have learned and narrow down the hypotheses. By asking pointed questions, the facilitator guides them to think about the implications of what they have learned and whether more investigation is needed. In medical school, the investigation can take place over several days.

In adapting the PBL approach to high school, care has to be taken to choose good questions for students to investigate (Hmelo-Silver, 2004). The problems should be realistic, open-ended, and resonant with student experience. For example, one class worked on planning a long trip on the Appalachian Trail, which involves learning about planning, fitness, geography, climate, expenses, and supplies that will be needed for the trip. Good facilitators model learning and thinking strategies for the students as they work on their plan. Teachers need to encourage students to explain their thinking as they work. The whiteboard technique mentioned earlier helps focus students' attention and provides a public space for them to develop and organize their ideas. A critical role for the facilitator is to foster self-directed learning and self-assessment by the students.

Learning by Design. Janet Kolodner has applied the PBL approach, together with "cognitive apprenticeship," to teach middle school science in a program she calls Learning by Design, which is embedded in a published curriculum called Project-Based Inquiry Science (Kolodner, 2007; Kolodner et al., 2003). At the beginning of the year, the students start with a launcher unit in order to learn the rituals they will be participating in as they take on new challenges. The launcher unit starts with an easy challenge, such as determining the best angle for a slope to launch a car over a flat terrain. Students work in small groups, conducting experiments to find their answer, after which each group presents its solution to the other students, who question them about how they did their experiment. Then the groups repeat their experiments and presentations, until they reach consensus on the experimental procedure and the answer to the challenge posed. As they work, they fill out a diary on their experiment, where they specify what they want to find out, what they predict, their experimental plan, a step-by-step procedure, the data they collect, a data summary, and a statement of what they learned. This reflection process is critical to learning to be systematic in how they carry out experiments.

In a more advanced unit, Vehicles in Motion, students are given the grand challenge of designing a car to go as far as possible over a hilly terrain. To meet this challenge, they go through repeated cycles of design and experimentation, addressing ever-more-difficult challenges. The groups begin to study different propulsion systems, such as a balloon-powered car and a rubber band–powered car. They run experiments on the different elements in their designs and other factors, such as friction from the terrain. In each cycle of design and experimentation, they make presentations to other students on both their proposed designs and their experiments. They face questions from other students and the teacher on why they made different decisions, and they learn from these discussions how to tackle different problems that arise.

As in PBL, they work with a whiteboard to present their designs and plans and to report their experimental results. The teacher's role follows the "cognitive apprenticeship" guidelines of modeling, coaching, scaffolding, and fading of support, and encouraging students to articulate their ideas clearly and to reflect on how they could do better (Collins, Brown & Holum, 1991; Collins, Brown, & Newman, 1989).

Computer-Simulation Environments. David Shaffer (2004, 2005, 2006) has developed computer-simulation environments to teach high school students the practices of professionals in different careers. He and his graduate students study how students in different professions are taught, in order to develop simulation-learning environments to mimic the strategies used to teach professionals. They have developed activities and simulations for science journalism, urban design, medicine, and engineering design that foster the practices, values, interests, and beliefs of people in different professions. For example, in their urban design activity, students are asked to use a geographic information system (GIS) to redesign an urban street, given the views of different constituents in the area, such as residents and store owners. Shaffer's goal is not to turn students into professionals, but rather to let them experience how knowledge and action are integrated in different professions to solve problems. His approach brings home how the knowledge students are learning is useful in solving real-world problems.

Roger Schank and his colleagues (Schank, Fano, Bell, & Jona, 1994) have developed simulations called goal-based scenarios that emphasize students solving real-world problems. One such simulation teaches genetics by having learners try to determine if couples are likely to have children with a genetic disease. In order to advise the couples, learners must find out how different genetic combinations lead to the disease and run tests to determine the parents' genetic makeup. There are scaffolds in the system to support the learners, such as various recorded experts who offer advice. Other simulations support learners in a wide variety of challenging tasks, such as solving an environmental problem or putting together a news broadcast about a historical event. These simulations make it possible to embed cognitive skills and knowledge in the kinds of contexts where they are to be used. So people learn not only the basic competencies they will need, but also when and how to apply these competencies.

Maker Movement. Recent years have seen an explosion of efforts (Peppler, Halverson, & Kafai, 2016) to engage students in schools, computer clubhouses, and museums in making things of interest to them using technology like computers and 3-D printers. The maker movement has kids designing a variety of products, such as jewelry, electronic clothing, movies, robots, and games. It provides an impetus for kids to learn entrepreneurial, engineering, and design skills that will be invaluable as they make their way in a changing world. The Digital Youth Network and Globaloria, described in Chapter 2, are examples of how the maker movement is being implemented in schools. In many settings adults and children work together to develop designs and products they can be proud of, involving science, technology, engineering, and the arts. This is the kind of collaborative education that helps kids develop identities as life-long learners and producers.

Schools need to build on models like these to prepare students to function in the complex society they are entering. The rest of the chapter shows how these elements can be brought together to address the kinds of issues that are important for students to grapple with in school.

A VISION FOR A 21ST-CENTURY SCHOOL

I envision a "passion school" where students of different ages work together on investigations and projects that are of real interest and value to the students. The distinctive aspect of the school is that children, with the help of their parents, choose the topical focus of the curricula in which they participate. In such a school, students are not segregated into grades, nor are they evaluated by taking tests. Students are not competing to look smart. Rather, all students are working to help their group accomplish tasks they have helped formulate. They are engaged in "personalized learning," similar to what AltSchools emphasize. There is an inevitable tension in such a school, as in the community-of-learners school Barbara Rogoff (1994) describes, between developing students' agency and making sure they learn the knowledge, skills, and dispositions they will need as adults.

School Design

When students enter the school at about 5 or 6 years old, they and their parents decide together on two curricula that students will participate in for half a day each. They choose among curriculum topics that are designed to appeal to young children. For example, possible topics might include family, vehicles, pets, dinosaurs, the sun, the moon and stars, toys, sports and games, and bugs—that is, whatever topics cover the range of things young children are interested in. Judy Harris Helm (2015) emphasizes the importance of choosing topics that children are familiar with, so they can bring their own experience to their investigations and are not dependent simply on what they read in books. Children might participate in a number of these curricula, each for 2 to 3 years from age 5 to 10 or 11.

The goal would be to embed literacy, math, science, history, geography, the arts, finance, health, the environment, and law in tasks the students work on in each of the curricula. It will take careful curriculum design to select projects that together involve all these important aspects of curriculum. For example, investigations and projects for students in the dinosaur curriculum might involve the following:

- Building a timeline of when different dinosaurs lived
- Developing a theory of why the dinosaurs disappeared
- Designing a dinosaur zoo and how it would run
- Building Lego Mindstorms dinosaurs that can move around and interact
- Comparing the size and characteristics of meat-eating and plant-eating dinosaurs
- Developing a world map of where different dinosaur skeletons have been found
- Investigating whether and how birds descended from dinosaurs
- Describing the environments where different dinosaurs lived
- Investigating the possibility and wisdom of regenerating dinosaurs from their DNA
- Developing legal guidelines for the sale of newly found dinosaur skeletons

The projects require students to read; write; do math; learn history, science, and engineering design; and program and model as appropriate in the context of the curriculum. There are endless possibilities for developing projects that children who are interested in dinosaurs would find challenging and educational.

The products of such investigations can take many different forms, just as Central Park East Secondary School encourages. They should include videos, debates, charts and graphs, op-ed articles, stories, proposals, blogs, graphic designs, artworks, simulations and games, spreadsheets, PowerPoint presentations, and other genres. As in the Digital Youth Network projects described in Chapter 2 (Barron, Gomez, Pinkard, & Martin, 2014), there should be an online network where students can post their work and other students can critique it.

As students grow older, curricula should reflect the kinds of occupations adults engage in, as David Shaffer has developed in his curriculum designs

described above. In this way, the curricula evolve to address the kind of topics seen in career academies, such as the New York School of the Performing
Arts, Bronx High School of Science, and Brooklyn Tech, all in New York
City. Over their school years, students might participate in eight to ten different curricula in total. For example, in later years, curricula might involve
the following areas pointing toward careers in different areas:

- *Life*—medicine, biology, pharmaceuticals, agriculture,
  bioengineering, gardening, environmental services, forestry
- *Engineering*—technology, computers, design, civil engineering,
  electrical engineering, technicians, atmospheric sciences, chemicals,
  geology, mining
- *Economics*—business, finance, retail, banking, manufacturing,
  construction, distribution
- *Government*—law, criminal justice, police, fire, social services,
  military, politics
- *Creativity*—music, video, dance, theater, art, architecture, design,
  interior decoration, writing
- *People*—social services, human resources, management, psychology,
  counseling, teaching, sociology, anthropology

My student Diana Joseph implemented some of the ideas for a passion
curriculum in an inner-city Chicago elementary school (Collins, Joseph, &
Bielaczyc, 2004). She chose the making of video documentaries as a context
to develop the curriculum design. Video is intrinsically interesting to the
late elementary students with whom she worked, and so provided a good
context for her design work. She created a system of certificates for students
in a variety of areas, such as scriptwriting, interviewing, and camera operation, based on the Scout merit badge system. She interwove important skills
and concepts into the video curriculum, such as math skills in the context of
budgeting, writing skills in scriptwriting, and planning skills in the development of a documentary. At the same time, there was an emphasis on learning content around the topic of each video students developed. For example,
in a documentary on immigration, there was an emphasis on historical and
geographical content. By engaging in work on projects they cared about,
students were willing to spend time on tedious details that they try to avoid
with schoolwork.

This structure for schooling allows for a true cognitive apprenticeship
to be developed, where there is an emphasis on students learning important
content and skills in the context of carrying out complex tasks. We have
developed a four-stage model for a cognitive apprenticeship in a passion
curriculum:

1. Students come in as novices and work on a project of their own,
    with one of the more experienced students mentoring them as they
    carry out the project.
2. As they gain experience, they begin to work on larger projects
    with other students, where more advanced students serve as
    project and subproject leaders.
3. After they have worked on a number of different projects, they are
    ready to serve as a mentor for a new incoming student.
4. After they have done their mentoring successfully, they are
    ready to begin serving as a project or subproject leader on larger
    projects.

This is a wholly new way to think about classroom organization.

In this model, students will be working in rich technological environments, which reflect the way technologies are used in the real world. Much
of the information they gather will be found on the Internet as well as in
books. Children are growing up surrounded by technology, and schools must
find a way to accommodate and enforce its responsible use by children, as
the AltSchools try to do. Classes will look much like those in schools where
group project work is emphasized.

The goal of the passion school design is to develop a community of
learners who are working together to address meaningful questions, sharing
knowledge and taking responsibility for completing the challenges they face.
The role of the teacher is to mentor students, posing challenges that will
help them learn the kinds of knowledge, skills, and dispositions needed for
a productive life, and working with the students as they grapple with these
challenges. There should be an emphasis on students developing expertise,
sharing what they learn, developing deep understanding of issues and ideas,
decisionmaking based on evidence, setting and meeting expectations, and
utilizing the humanities, arts, and natural and social sciences as ways of
understanding and affecting the world.

Embedding Knowledge, Skills, and Dispositions into Curricula

The fundamental way that the new literacy discussed in Chapter 2 can be
embedded into different curricula is to have students produce works in many
different genres that they post on a network for other students to learn from
and critique. The network might include videos of performances, such as
plays, debates, documentaries, animations, artistic performances, and presentations. Students might write blogs, op-eds, news reports and analyses,
stories like those on fan fiction sites, poems, and memoirs. They might design

simulations, educational games, representations of phenomena in the world, redesigns of places in their town or city, new laws and regulations, and guides such as how to create animé characters in Scratch (Resnick et al., 2009). Just as in the Digital Youth Network and Rogoff's community-of-learners school, it would be good to have parents and mentors from the neighborhood come in during or after school to help students with their projects.

How are students to learn about and develop all the different aspects of self-reliance discussed in Chapter 3? In particular, they need to understand health, financial, and legal matters, and develop capabilities for strategic thinking; self-control; planning, monitoring, and reflecting; and flexible adaptation.

To address the topic of health in a curriculum on family, students might plan family dinners for a month, taking into consideration dietary and health issues; they might analyze different sports and activities in terms of their exercise value; and they might identify the different stresses that arise in family life. For a curriculum on economics, students might look at the costs and benefits of the food system in the country with respect to people's health, and how to change incentive systems so that people get more exercise and less stress. Similarly, financial and legal issues arise in many different contexts, in developing budgets and legal agreements. By addressing these topics in different curricula, students see how they apply in different contexts.

An emphasis on strategic thinking and planning, monitoring, and reflecting on their work should pervade every aspect of what students do in school. As students take up each challenge, they should plan their work using something like the PBL whiteboard. Keeping a structured diary as in Learning by Design will help them reflect on their work. Teachers can foster monitoring by circulating among the groups, asking what they are trying to do and if they are making progress. The goal of this questioning is for students to learn to ask themselves these questions as they work. Strategic thinking arises as they learn to solve problems working with different students and facing questions when they make presentations. Self-control develops as they work to meet deadlines and try to recover from things that go wrong. A main goal in having students work on challenging projects is to develop adaptability to the difficulties they encounter and the opportunities that arise.

In Chapter 4, we described some of the skills students will need in the workplaces of the 21st century, including creative and critical thinking, managing time and resources, and working with others in teams. These skills should be interwoven throughout the investigations and projects in which students engage. Teachers should encourage students to use a variety of creative thinking strategies, such as case comparison, perspective shifting, and looking for analogies, as they develop their ideas and designs for their projects. Similarly, teachers should encourage critical thinking by getting students to systematically critique ideas and products that they and others produce, and to perform cost-benefit analyses as they develop different proposed solutions to problems that arise.

Time-management skills are learned in the context of working to complete investigations and projects on time, particularly when students take on the role of project manager. Project managers have to coordinate different students' work so that everything fits together and is finished in a timely manner. Resource-management skills arise as students put together portfolios of their work to be used to evaluate how well they are doing. As students acquire a large portfolio of work over their school careers, indexing becomes critical for retrieval and reuse. Because the students are working in groups on many of their projects, they will have to learn the skills of listening to others' ideas and helping their groups work together successfully to create good products. Teachers can encourage cooperative work habits by having students use the kinds of managerial guides developed by Barbara White and by having students develop social norms as described in Chapter 2.

Chapter 5 addresses public policy challenges as examples of complex systems. I suggested that students might investigate the environmental and economic issues raised in the chapter using a problem-based learning (PBL) approach. For example, they might address the problem of feeding 11 billion people while dealing with issues such as genetically modified plants, supplies of fresh water, the chemical pollution produced by farming, the health effects of agricultural practices, and the treatment of animals in industrial farming. Similarly, they might address economic issues, such as how the banking system works, saving and compound interest, how to make markets work more efficiently, factors that affect the prices of goods, and how incentive systems can be used to solve societal problems. These kinds of questions can be addressed in many different curricula.

In Chapter 6, I addressed the math and science concepts that are central to dealing with the issues students will face in their adult years. Janet Kolodner has shown us how to embed mathematical and scientific thinking into projects that engage students in meaningful learning. Alane Starko and Gina Schack (1992), in their book *Looking for Data in All the Right Places*, describe studies that young children can carry out to address issues they care about. For example, students in a family curriculum might study how a baby changes over the school year, keeping a record of all their observations and measurements of the baby. For a pets or bugs curriculum, they suggest a longitudinal study of a gerbil or insect where students record data on the animal from birth to death. They describe how to collect survey data from other children on their favorite sports, pets, or other family members. And they detail how young children can analyze their data, create graphs and charts, and conduct statistical tests.

A major goal of a passion school should be to teach students how to interpret and create representations of theories and data. Michelle Wilkerson has been developing activities and computer tools to help children learn to create their own representations of data (Wilkerson-Jerde & Laina, 2015). For example, she had middle school children work with data sets from their city, showing how land use and population have changed over time. Students were encouraged to create representations that show how their city has changed. One group of girls wanted to show that minorities were not increasing as much as the press implied, and so they created 100 stick figures in four different colors representing the population at three different times. The representation showed that the number of minorities was increasing, but that minorities were still a small percentage of the population. The girls were learning to make an argument using data as evidence. This is critical to learning how to mathematize phenomena in the world.

In the brief summary of possible projects in the dinosaur curriculum, I suggested several representations (such as timelines, comparison tables, and world maps) that students might use to represent their findings. In Chapter 6, I tried to show that scientists use many different representations to capture their theories, and I think students similarly should learn to use equations, simulations, and trend analyses—for example, to represent the phenomena they are investigating, in order to make compelling arguments. Students who think they don't like math, science, or history will find themselves involved in projects that require the use of these disciplines to accomplish their project goals. The ability to develop convincing data to make arguments is becoming central to success in the modern world.

Different topics covered in this book can be embedded in multiple curricula. Not every topic will fit easily in every curriculum, but by engaging in different curricula, students should all come to understand the important ideas they will need as adults.

Assessing Students

Students can be assessed at three different levels: badges, portfolios, and graduation requirements like those at Central Park East Secondary School. Badges represent a movement that is spreading among nonschool environments, such as the Digital Youth Network, to certify specific skills students acquire outside of school (Casilli & Hickey, 2016; O'Byrne, Schenke, Willis, & Hickey, 2015). They might document that a student has mastered PowerPoint or is producing digital graphics. Diana Joseph experimented with badges when she had her students working for certificates in script-writing, interviewing, and camera operation. Schools might develop rubrics for different badges that students could earn as they work on their projects. There might be badges for developing budgets, managing work teams, or producing simulations in NetLogo. The virtue of badges is to document specific skills that students have mastered, rather than the vague generalities that grades and SAT scores represent.

Many schools have adopted portfolios to document the work students do over the course of the year. Having students record their work online makes it much easier to collect their work in portfolios that they can carry with them throughout their school careers. Offline work can be scanned into computers, and performances can be recorded with online video. Because much of a student's work will be done with other students, it is important that the teacher and students specify the contributions of different group members for each project. Portfolios provide a way for schools to communicate with parents and other outsiders, such as potential employers, what the students have accomplished. Reports to parents should include students' reflections on their work as well as teacher evaluations.

One virtue of portfolios is to show the different kinds of work that students have done and students' growth over the years. Students can take pride in showing off their best work and the response of others to their work. By selecting their best work to include in the portfolio, they are encouraged to critique their own work. This can foster efforts to improve in the areas where they find their work to be weaker.

The graduation requirements developed at Central Park East Secondary School give students direction to point to as they collect badges and put together their portfolios. The 14 areas that CPESS required students to address are a good place to start. Requiring students to defend their work before a committee ensures that they understand the implications of their work and did not depend on others (such as parents or other students) to complete their projects. Students should have an advisor for each of the areas to guide them in putting together a portfolio that demonstrates their competence. They should spend the final 2 years of school putting together their portfolios for graduation.

Assessment in school should not require passing tests. Tests put students in competition, producing winners and losers. And they reduce what is taught to those skills that can be easily tested. If we want schools to emphasize the knowledge, skills, and dispositions that are critical for thriving in the 21st century, we have to abandon the mass testing that has been emphasized in recent years. Badges, portfolios, and graduation requirements make it possible to assess students in a way that protects them from feeling stupid and emphasizes the development of deep knowledge and skills in a wide variety of areas.

SCHOOLS OF THE FUTURE

It is possible to create schools where students are engaged in pursuing meaningful activities and where teachers are rewarded with the pleasure of mentoring students as they learn the knowledge, skills, and dispositions that will help them thrive as adults. Such schools will be very different from traditional schools where students are doing what they are told, filling out worksheets, and being punished for misbehaving because they do not like the regimen imposed on them.

Like the school Barbara Rogoff (1994) describes, schools can be created where students love to go. Such schools cannot be competitive places where a few students shine and most students look bad by comparison. Students must work together to accomplish tasks they see value in pursuing. Activities must be built on students' natural interests. Students are willing to do difficult work when they understand why they are doing it. And to understand why, they must see the goal they are pursuing as worth their effort—not simply to please their teacher or parents, but to please themselves. Investigations and projects give students time to invest themselves in what they produce.

Mentoring students who are engaged in meaningful activities is very rewarding for teachers. In such settings, teachers do not have to spend all their time trying to make sure students behave, because students are too engaged to misbehave. Learning how to mentor wisely will take a different kind of teacher education, but it does not require learning a lot of facts and procedures. Instead, it requires a willingness to learn along with students. It also requires learning the kinds of knowledge, skills, and dispositions I have outlined in the book.

How do we get there from here? The charter school and micro-school movements provide a mechanism for schools to experiment with new designs. High Tech Schools, Summit Public Schools, and AltSchools are experimenting with many of these ideas. These school models may spread widely across America. Educational designers and researchers should work together and learn from one another. Researchers should get behind these school design efforts, to push the thinking forward and as venues for carrying out investigations in a world where real learning can happen. Partnerships between learning scientists and school designers are needed to redesign schooling for the 21st century.

As parents demand more charter schools and as educators see which ones are most successful in engaging students and attracting effective teachers, schooling may evolve toward a model that better prepares students for the world they are entering. I hope these proposals will influence the design of charter schools and micro-schools as these movements grow. Ideally, the passion school vision will inspire educational leaders to experiment with new designs and develop schools where students are engaged and work together to accomplish meaningful goals.

REFERENCES

Abeles, V. (2015). *Beyond measure: Rescuing an overscheduled, overtested, under-estimated generation.* New York, NY: Simon & Schuster.

Anderson, J. R. (1993). *Rules of the mind.* Hillsdale, NJ: Lawrence Erlbaum.

Barron, B. (2000). Achieving coordination in collaborative problem-solving groups. *Journal of the Learning Sciences, 9*(4), 403–436.

Barron, B. (2003). When smart groups fail. *Journal of the Learning Sciences, 12*(3), 307–359.

Barron, B. (2006). Interest and self-sustained learning as catalysts of development: A learning ecologies perspective. *Human Development, 49*(4), 193–224.

Barron, B., Gomez, K., Pinkard, N., & Martin, C. (2014). *The Digital Youth Network: Cultivating new media citizenship in urban communities.* Cambridge, MA: MIT Press.

Barrows, H. S., & Tamblyn R. M. (1980). *Problem based learning.* New York, NY: Springer.

Basch, C. E. (2011). Physical activity and the achievement gap among urban minority youth. *Journal of School Health, 81*(10), 626–634.

Baumeister, R. G., & Tierney, J. (2011). *Willpower: Rediscovering the greatest human strength.* New York, NY: Penguin.

Bazelon, E. (2013). *Sticks and stones: Defeating the culture of bullying and rediscovering the power of character and empathy.* New York, NY: Random House.

Benezet, L. P. (1991, May). The teaching of arithmetic: The story of an experiment. *Humanistic Mathematics Newsletter, 6,* 2–14.

Bielaczyc, K., & Collins, A. (1999). Learning communities in classrooms: A reconceptualization of educational practice. In C. M. Reigeluth (Ed.), *Instructional-design theories and models: A new paradigm of instructional theory* (pp. 269–292). Mahwah, NJ: Lawrence Erlbaum.

Bielaczyc, K., Kapur, M., & Collins, A. (2013). Cultivating a community of learners in K–12 classrooms. In C. E. Hmelo-Silver, A. M. O'Donnell, C. A. Chinn, & C. Chan (Eds.), *International handbook of collaborative learning* (pp. 233–249). New York, NY: Routledge.

Black, R. W. (2009). English-language learners, fan communities, and 21st century skills. *Journal of Adolescent & Adult Literacy, 52*(8), 688–697.

Borge, M., Yan, S., Shimoda, T., & Toprani, D. (in press). Moving beyond making: Towards the development of ThinkerSpaces. Proceedings of CHI2016

(San Jose, California, May 7–12). Retrieved from hci.sbg.ac.at/wp-content /uploads/2015/11/Moving_Beyond_Making.pdf

Bransford, J. D., Brown, A. L., & Cocking, R. (2000). *How people learn: Brain, mind, experience and school* (Expanded ed.). Washington, DC: National Academies Press.

Bransford, J. D., Franks, J. J., Vye, N. J., & Sherwood, R. D. (1989). New approaches to instruction: Because wisdom can't be told. In S. Vosniadou & A. Ortony (Eds.), *Similarity and analogical reasoning* (pp. 470–497). New York, NY: Cambridge University Press.

Brick, M. (2010, May 20). Texas school board set to vote textbook revisions. *New York Times*. Retrieved from www.nytimes.com/2010/05/21/education/21textbooks .html.

Brooks, A. K. (1994). Power and the production of knowledge: Collective team learning in work organizations. *Human Resource Development Quarterly, 5*(3), 213–235.

Brown, J. S., & Thomas, D. (2006, April). You play *World of Warcraft*? You're hired! *Wired* 14.04. Retrieved from www.wired.com/2006/04/learn/

Bruckman, A. (2000). Situated support for learning: Storm's weekend with Rachael. *Journal of the Learning Sciences, 9*(3), 329–372.

Brynjolfsson, E., & McAfee, A. (2014). *The second machine age: Work, progress, and prosperity in a time of brilliant technologies.* New York, NY: Norton.

Burger, E. B., & Starbird, M. (2013). *The five elements of effective thinking.* Princeton, NJ: Princeton University Press.

Callahan, R. E. (1962). *Education and the cult of efficiency.* Chicago, IL: University of Chicago Press.

Carr, N. (2011). *The shallows: What the Internet is doing to our brains.* New York, NY: W. W. Norton.

Casilli C., & Hickey, D. T. (2016). Transcending conventional credentialing and assessment paradigms with information-rich digital badges. *The Information Society, 32*(2), 117–129.

Cohen, E. G. (1994). *Designing groupwork: Strategies for the heterogenous classroom* (2nd ed.). New York, NY: Teachers College Press.

Collins, A. (2011). A study of expert theory formation: The role of model types and domain frameworks. In M. S. Khine & I. Saleh (Eds.), *Models and modeling: Cognitive tools for scientific enquiry* (pp. 23–40). London, England: Springer.

Collins, A., Brown, J. S., & Holum, A. (1991, Winter). Cognitive apprenticeship: Making thinking visible. *American Educator, 15*(3), 6–11, 38–46.

Collins, A., Brown, J. S., & Newman, S. E. (1989). Cognitive apprenticeship: Teaching the crafts of reading, writing, and mathematics. In L. B. Resnick (Ed.), *Knowing, learning, and instruction: Essays in honor of Robert Glaser* (pp. 453–494). Hillsdale, NJ: Lawrence Erlbaum.

Collins, A., & Ferguson, W. (1993). Epistemic forms and epistemic games: Structures and strategies to guide inquiry. *Educational Psychologist, 28*(1), 25–42.

Collins, A., & Gentner, D. (1980). A framework for a cognitive theory of writing. In L. W. Gregg & E. Steinberg (Eds.), *Cognitive processes in writing: An interdisciplinary approach* (pp. 51–72). Hillsdale, NJ: Lawrence Erlbaum.

Collins, A., & Halverson, R. (2009). *Rethinking education in the age of technology: The digital revolution and schooling in America.* New York, NY: Teachers College Press.

Collins, A., & Halverson, R. (2015). The functionality of literacy in a digital world. In R. J. Spiro, M. DeSchryver, P. Morsink, M. Schira-Hagerman, & P. Thompson (Eds.), *Reading at a crossroads? Disjunctures and continuities in our conceptions and practices of reading in the 21st century* (pp. 172–179). New York, NY: Routledge.

Collins, A., Joseph, D., & Bielaczyc, K. (2004). Design research: Theoretical and methodological issues. *Journal of the Learning Sciences, 13*(1), 15–42.

Collins, A., Neville, P., & Bielaczyc, K. (2000). The role of different media in designing learning environments. *International Journal of Artificial Intelligence in Education, 11,* 144–162.

Collins, A., & White, B. Y. (2015). How technology is broadening the nature of learning dialogues. In L. B. Resnick, C. S. C. Asterhan, & S. N. Clarke (Eds.), *Socializing intelligence through academic talk and dialogue* (pp. 225–233). Washington, DC: AERA Books.

Cremin, L. A. (1951). *The American common school: An historic conception.* New York, NY: Columbia University Teachers College.

Cremin, L. A. (1980). *American education: The national experience 1783–1876.* New York, NY: Harper & Row.

Crowley, C., & Lodge, H. S. (2004). *Younger next year: Live strong, fit, and sexy—until you're 80 and beyond.* New York, NY: Workman.

Cuban, L. (2001). *Oversold and underused: Computers in the classroom.* Cambridge, MA: Harvard University Press.

Daiute, C. (1985). *Writing and computers.* Reading, MA: Addison-Wesley.

Darling-Hammond, L., Ancess, J., & Falk, B. (1995). *Authentic assessment in action: Studies of schools and students at work.* New York, NY: Teachers College Press.

Dawkins, R. (1976). *The selfish gene.* Oxford, England: Oxford University Press.

Devlin, K. (2012). *Introduction to mathematical thinking.* Palo Alto, CA: Author.

Dementia. (2015). Retrieved from my.clevelandclinic.org/health/articles/types-of-dementia

Diener, E., & Biswas-Diener, R. (2008). *Happiness: Unlocking the mysteries of psychological wealth.* Malden, MA: Blackwell.

Donnellon, A. (1995). *Team talk: The power of language in team dynamics.* Boston, MA: Harvard Business School Press.

Dunbar, K. (1993). Concept discovery in a scientific domain. *Cognitive Science, 17*(3), 397–434.

Dweck, C. (2008). *Mindset: The new psychology of success.* New York, NY: Ballantine.

8

References

Ehrlich, P. R. (1971). *The population bomb*. New York, NY: Ballantine.

Eisenhower, D. D. (1957). Remarks at the National Defense Executive Reserve Conference, November 14, 1957. Retrieved from the American Presidency Project website: www.presidency.ucsb.edu/ws/?pid=10951.

Fisher, R., Ury, W., & Patton, B. (1991). *Getting to yes: Negotiating agreement without giving in* (2nd ed.). New York, NY: Penguin.

Flynn, J. R. (1999). Searching for justice: The discovery of IQ gains over time. *American Psychologist, 54,* 5–20.

Friedman, M., & Schwartz, A. J. (1963). *A monetary history of the United States, 1867–1960*. Princeton, NJ: Princeton University Press.

Friedman, T. L. (2004). *The world is flat: A brief history of the twenty-first century*. New York, NY: Farrar, Straus and Giroux.

Gee, J. P. (2003). *What video games have to teach us about learning and literacy*. New York, NY: Palgrave Macmillan.

Graham, J., Christian, L., & Kiecolt-Glaser, J. (2006). Stress, age, and immune function: Toward a lifespan approach. *Journal of Behavioral Medicine, 29,* 389–400.

Guise, S. (2015). *How to be an imperfectionist: The new way to self-acceptance, fearless living, and freedom from perfectionism*. Columbus, OH: Selective Entertainment.

Gurian, P. (Producer), & Coppola, F. F. (Director). (1986). *Peggy Sue got married* (Film). Los Angeles, CA: TriStar Pictures.

Halpern, D. F. (1998). Teaching critical thinking for transfer across domains: Dispositions, skills, structure training, and metacognitive monitoring. *American Psychologist, 53*(4), 449–455.

Hammer, M., & Hershman, L. W. (2010). *Faster cheaper better: The 9 levers for transforming how work gets done*. New York, NY: Crown Business.

Hardin, G. (1968). The tragedy of the commons. *Science, 162*(3859), 1243–1248.

Hatano, G., & Inagaki, K. (1986). Two courses of expertise. In H. W. Stevenson, H. Azuma, & K. Hakuta (Eds.), *Child development and education in Japan* (pp. 262–272). New York, NY: W. H. Freeman.

Heath, S. B., & Mangiola, L. (1991). *Children of promise: Literate activity in linguistically and culturally diverse classrooms*. Washington, DC: National Education Association.

Helm, J. H. (2015) *Becoming young thinkers: Deep project work in the classroom*. New York, NY: Teachers College Press.

Hirsch, E. D., Jr. (1987). *Cultural literacy: What every American needs to know*. Boston, MA: Houghton Mifflin.

Hmelo-Silver, C. E. (2004). Problem-based learning: What and how do students learn? *Educational Psychology Review, 16*(3), 235–266.

Hsi, S., & Hoadley, C. M. (1997). Productive discussion in science: Gender equity through electronic discourse. *Journal of Science Education and Technology, 6*(1), 23–36.

Jenkins, H. (2008). *Convergence culture: Where old and new media collide.* New York, NY: NYU Press.

Johnson, S. (2010). *Where good ideas come from: The natural history of innovation.* New York, NY: Penguin.

Jung, Y., & Borge, M. (2016). Problems with different interests of learners in an informal CSCL setting. In C. K. Looi, J. L. Polman, U. Cress, & P. Reimann (Eds.), *Transforming learning, empowering learners: The International Conference of the Learning Sciences (ICLS) 2016, Volume 1* (pp. 878–881). Singapore: International Society of the Learning Sciences.

Kapur, M. (2008). Productive failure. *Cognition and Instruction, 26*(3), 379–424.

Kapur, M., & Bielaczyc, K. (2011). Designing for productive failure. *Journal of the Learning Sciences, 21*(1), 45–83.

Knobel, M. (2008, April). *Studying anime music video remix as a new literacy.* Paper presented at the Annual Meeting of the American Educational Research Association, New York, NY.

Kolodner, J. L. (2007). The roles of scripts in promoting collaborative discourse in Learning by Design. In F. Fisher, I. Kollar, H. Mandl, & J. M. Haake (Eds.), *Scripting computer-based collaborative learning.* (pp. 237–262). New York, NY: Springer.

Kolodner, J. L., Camp, P. J., Crismond, D., Fasse, B., Gray, J., Holbrook, J., Puntambekar, S., & Ryan, M. (2003). Problem-based learning meets case-based reasoning in the middle-school classroom: Putting Learning by Design into practice. *Journal of the Learning Sciences, 12*(4), 495–547.

Konnikova, M. (2014, October 9). The struggles of a psychologist studying self-control. *The New Yorker.* Retrieved from www.newyorker.com/science/maria-konnikova/struggles-psychologist-studying-self-control

Leander, K., & Boldt, G. (2008). *New literacies in old literacy skins.* Paper presented at the Annual Meeting of the American Educational Research Association, New York, NY.

Lehrer, J. (2009, May 18). Don't: The secret of self-control. *New Yorker.* Retrieved from www.newyorker.com/magazine/2009/05/18/dont-2

Lehrer, R., & Schauble, L. (2006). Cultivating model-based reasoning in science education. In R. K. Sawyer (Ed.), *The handbook of the learning sciences.* New York, NY: Cambridge University Press.

Leu, D. J. (2010, April). *The new literacies of online reading comprehension: Recent and ongoing research.* Paper presented at the annual conference of the American Educational Research Association, Denver, CO.

Lewis, C. (2007). New literacies. In M. Knobel & C. Lankshear (Eds.), *A new literacies sampler* (pp. 229–238). New York, NY: Peter Lang.

Lippert, M. (2009). Organic—or not? Is organic produce healthier than traditional? *Eating Well.com.* Retrieved from www.eatingwell.com/food_news_origins/green_sustainable/organic_or_not_is_organic_produce_healthier_than_conventional

126

References

Mandinach, E. B., & Cline, H. F. (2013). *Classroom dynamics: Implementing a technology-based learning environment*. New York, NY: Routledge.

Markoff, J. (2011, February 16). Computer wins on '*Jeopardy!*': Trivial, it's not. *New York Times*. Retrieved from www.nytimes.com/2011/02/17/science/17jeopardy-watson.html?pagewanted=all&_r=0

Meadows, D. H. (1999). *Leverage points: Places to intervene in a system*. Hartland, VT: Sustainability Institute. Retrieved from www.fraw.org.uk/files/limits/meadows_1999.pdf

Meadows, D. H. (2008). *Thinking in systems*. White River Junction, VT: Chelsea Green Publishing.

Meier, D. (1995). *The power of their ideas*. Boston, MA: Beacon Press.

Michaels, S., O'Connor, C., & Resnick, L. B. (2008). Deliberative discourse idealized and realized: Accountable talk in the classroom and in civic life. *Studies in Philosophy and Education, 27*(4), 283–297.

Mischel, W. (2014). *The marshmallow test: Why self-control is the engine of success*. New York, NY: Little Brown.

National Heart, Lung, and Blood Institute. (2012). What causes overweight and obesity? Retrieved from www.nhlbi.nih.gov/health/health-topics/topics/obe/causes

Neary, L. (2011, March 28). Children's book apps: A new world of learning. Retrieved from www.npr.org/2011/03/28/134663712/childrens-book-apps-a-new-world-of-learning

Newell, A., & Simon, H. A. (1972). *Human problem solving*. Englewood Cliffs, NJ: Prentice-Hall.

O'Byrne, W. I., Schenke, K., Willis, J. E., & Hickey, D. T. (2015). Digital badges: Recognizing, assessing, and motivating learners in and out of school contexts. *Journal of Adolescent & Adult Literacy, 58*(6), 451–454.

Ophir, E., Nass, C., & Wagner, A. (2009). Cognitive control in media multitaskers. *Proceedings of the National Academy of Sciences, 106*(33), 15583–15587.

Packer, A. (1997). Mathematical competencies that employers expect. In L. A. Steen (Ed.), *Why numbers count: Quantitative literacy for tomorrow's America* (pp. 137–154). New York, NY: College Entrance Examination Board.

Papert, S. (1980). *Mindstorms: Children, computers and powerful ideas*. New York, NY: Basic Books.

Papert, S. (1997). *The children's machine: Rethinking school in the age of the computer*. New York, NY: Basic Books.

Park, A. (2016, April 8). Five facts that show the dismal state of school exercise programs. *Time Magazine*. Retrieved from time.com/4285702/5-facts-about-the-dismal-state-of-school-exercise-programs/

Pepper, C. (2012, December 11). Help students de-stress for success. *Edutopia*. Retrieved from www.edutopia.org/blog/help-students-de-stress-success

Peppler, K., Halverson, E. R., & Kafai, Y. B. (2016). *Makeology: Makers as learners* (vols. 1 & 2). New York, NY: Routledge.

Piety, P. J. (2013). *Assessing the educational data movement*. New York, NY: Teachers College Press.

Poe, M. T. (2011). *A history of communications: Media and society from the evolution of speech to the Internet*. New York, NY: Cambridge University Press.

Pollan, M. (2009). *Food rules: An eater's manual*. New York, NY: Penguin.

Postman, N. (1982). *The disappearance of childhood*. New York, NY: Delacorte.

Postman, N. (1985). *Amusing ourselves to death: Public discourse in the age of show business*. New York, NY: Penguin.

Powell, A. G., Farrar, E., & Cohen, D. K. (1985). *The shopping mall high school: Winners and losers in the educational marketplace*. Boston, MA: Houghton Mifflin.

Resnick, M., Maloney, J., Monroy-Hernández, A., Rusk, N., Eastmond, E., Brennan, K., Millner, A., Rosenbaum, E., Silver, J., Silverman, B., & Kafai, Y. (2009). Scratch: Programming for all. *Communications of the ACM, 52*(11), 60–67.

Robinson, K. (2010, October). *Ken Robinson: Changing education paradigms* [video]. Retrieved from www.ted.com/talks/ken_robinson_changing_education _paradigms

Rogoff, B. (1994). Developing understanding of the idea of communities of learners. *Mind, Culture, and Activity, 1*(4), 209–229.

Rosen, L. D. (2010). *Rewired: Understanding the iGeneration and the way they learn*. New York, NY: Palgrave Macmillan.

Sadler, P. M. (1987). Misconceptions in astronomy. In J. Novak (Ed.), *Misconceptions and educational strategies in science and mathematics* (pp. 422–437). Ithaca, NY: Cornell University Press.

Saxenian, A. (1999). *Silicon Valley's new immigrant entrepreneurs*. San Francisco, CA: Public Policy Institute of California.

SCANS Commission. (1991). *What work requires of schools: A SCANS Report for America 2000*. Washington, DC: The Secretary's Commission on Achieving Necessary Skills, U. S. Department of Labor.

Schank, R. C. (1988). *The creative attitude: Learning to ask and answer the right questions*. New York, NY: Macmillan.

Schank, R. C., Fano, A., Bell, B., & Jona, M. (1994). The design of goal-based scenarios. *Journal of the Learning Sciences, 3*(4), 305–346.

Schoenfeld, A. J. (1985). *Mathematical problem solving*. New York, NY: Academic Press.

Seligman, M. E. P. (1994). *What you can change . . . and what you can't: The complete guide to successful self-improvement*. New York, NY: Random House.

Shaffer, D. W. (2004). Pedagogical praxis: The professions as models for postindustrial education. *Teachers College Record, 106*(7), 1401–1421.

Shaffer, D. W. (2005). Epistemic games. *Innovate: Journal of Online Education, 1*(6), 2–6.

Shaffer, D. W. (2006). *How computer games help children learn*. New York, NY: Palgrave Macmillan.

Simon, H. A. (1969). *The sciences of the artificial*. Cambridge, MA: MIT Press.

Simon, J. L. (1980, June 27). Resources, population, environment: An oversupply of false bad news. *Science, 208*, 1431–1437.

Sinatra, S. T., & Roberts, J. C. (2007). *Reverse heart disease now: Stop deadly cardiovascular plaque before it's too late.* Hoboken, NJ: John Wiley & Sons.

Slichter, S. H. (1948). *The American economy: Its problems and prospects.* New York, NY: Knopf.

Stager, C. (2011). *Deep future: The next 100,000 years of life on earth.* New York, NY: St. Martin's Press.

Starko, A. J., & Schack, G. D. (1992). *Looking for data in all the right places: A guidebook for conducting original research with young children.* Mansfield Center, CT: Creative Learning Press.

Stigler, J., & Hiebert, J. (1999). *The teaching gap: Best ideas from the world's teachers for improving education in the classroom.* New York, NY: Free Press.

Toffler, A. (1980). *The third wave.* New York, NY: Bantam Books.

Trilling, B., & Fadel, C. (2009). *21st century skills: Learning for life in our times.* San Francisco, CA: Jossey-Bass.

Turkle, S. (2011). *Alone together: Why we expect more from technology and less from each other.* New York, NY: Basic Books.

Turkle, S. (2015). *Reclaiming conversation: The power of talk in a digital age.* New York, NY: Penguin.

Valverde, G. A., & Schmidt, W. H. (1997). Refocusing U. S. math and science education. *Issues in Science and Technology, 14*(2), 60–66.

Wagner, T. (2008). *The global achievement gap: Why even our best schools don't teach the new survival skills our children need—and what we can do about it.* New York, NY: Basic Books.

Waller, M. J., Conte, J. M., Gibson, C. B., & Carpenter, M. A. (2001). The effect of individual perception of deadlines on team performance. *Academy of Management Review, 4,* 586–600.

Warren, E., & Tyagi, A. W. (2003). *The two-income trap: Why middle-class parents are going broke.* New York, NY: Basic Books.

Weinberg, S. (2004, March). Crazy for history. *Journal of American History, 90,* 1401–1414.

White, B. Y., Collins, A., & Frederiksen, J. R. (2011). The nature of scientific metaknowledge. In M. S. Khine & I. Saleh (Eds.), *Models and modeling: Cognitive tools for scientific enquiry* (pp. 41–76). London, England: Springer.

White, B. Y., & Frederiksen, J. R. (1998). Inquiry, modeling, and metacognition: Making science accessible to all students. *Cognition and Instruction, 16*(1), 3–118.

White, B. Y., & Frederiksen, J. R. (2005). A theoretical framework and approach for fostering metacognitive development. *Educational Psychologist, 40*(4), 211–223.

White, B. Y., Frederiksen, J. R., & Collins, A. (2009). The interplay of scientific inquiry and metacognition: More than a marriage of convenience. In D. Hacker, J. Dunlosky, & A. Graesser (Eds.), *Handbook of metacognition in education* (pp. 175–205). New York, NY: Routledge.

Wilensky, U. (1999). GasLab: An extensible modeling toolkit for connecting micro- and macro-properties of gases. In W. Feurzeig & N. Roberts (Eds.), *Modeling and simulation in science and mathematics education* (pp. 151–178). New York, NY: Springer.

Wilensky, U., & Reisman, K. (2006). Thinking like a wolf, a sheep, or a firefly: Learning biology through constructing and testing computational theories—an embodied modeling approach. *Cognition and Instruction, 24*(2), 171–209.

Wilensky, U., & Resnick, M. (1999). Thinking in levels: A dynamic systems approach to making sense of the world. *Journal of Science Education and Technology, 8*(1), 3–19.

Wilkerson-Jerde, M., & Laina, V. (2015, January). *Stories of our city: Coordinating youths' mathematical, representational, and community knowledge through data visualization design.* Paper presented at the American Educational Research Association Conference, Chicago, IL.

Wilson, E. O. (2003). *The future of life.* New York, NY: Vintage.

Wiseman, F. (Producer & Director). (1994). *High school II* (Film). New York, NY: Zipporah Films.

Young, R. E., Becker, A. L., & Pike, K. L. (1970). *Rhetoric: Discovery and change.* New York, NY: Harcourt, Brace & World.

Zumbrum, J. (2015, April 8). Is your job "routine"? If so, it's probably disappearing. *Wall Street Journal.* Retrieved from blogs.wsj.com/economics/2015/04/08/is-your-job-routine-if-so-its-probably-disappearing/

INDEX

Abeles, Vicki, 5
Accountable talk (Michaels et al.), 26, 28
Adaptive expertise, 9, 51–52
Aerobic exercise, 40–41
Affinity spaces (Gee), 25
Africa, 81
After-school programs, 24, 107
Agent models, 98
Agriculture, 35, 56
Alliances, 47
Alone Together (Turkle), 26
AltSchools, 107, 111, 114, 119
Alzheimer's disease, 40
American Heart Association, 38–39
Analogies, 57–58, 59
Analysis of variance, 91
Ancess, J., 9–10, 14, 106
Anderson, J. R., 99
Anger management, 48
Artificial intelligence, 55, 58, 60, 84
Arts, 14
Assessment, 117–119
    badge systems, 113, 117–118
    graduation requirements, 14–15,
        105–106, 117, 118–119
    in passion schools, 117–119
    portfolios, 66, 105–107, 116–118
    rubrics, 5, 105, 118
    of teamwork, 72
    tests, 2, 4–6, 41, 49, 118–119
Asymptote, 87
Automation of work, 54–56, 84

Badge systems, 113, 117–118
Bankruptcy, 42–43
Barber, Benjamin, 34
Barbie Girls, 17
Bar graphs, 86

Barron, Brigid, 14, 20, 24, 68, 112
Barrows, Howard S., 72, 108–109
Basch, C. E., 41
Baumeister, Roy G., 48–49, 65
Bazelon, Emily, 45
Becker, Alton L., 58, 59
Behavioral models, 94, 98–99, 101
Beliefs, 9–10
Bell, B., 110
Benezet, L. P., 13
Bernstein, Seymour, 36
Between-subjects variables, 91
Bielaczyc, K., 29, 52, 68, 113
Binomial distribution, 88
Biswas-Diener, Robert, 47–48
Black, Rebecca W., 20
Blogs, 25, 56
Boldt, Gail, 21
Borge, Marcela, 30, 47
Brainstorming, 32
Bransford, John D., 51–52
Brennan, K., 20, 115
Brick, M., 3
Bronx High School of Science (New
    York), 113
Brooklyn Tech (New York), 113
Brooks, Ann K., 67–69
Brown, A. L., 51–52
Brown, John Seely, ix–x, 21, 110
Bruckman, Amy, 19
Brynjolfsson, Eric, 55
Bubbles, 76–77
Bullying, 25, 38, 45
Burger, Edward B., 62–63

Callahan, Raymond E., 3
Camp, P. J., 51, 109–110
Cancer, 40

Caperton, Idit Harel, 23–24
Career skills, 54–69. *See also* Self-
    sufficiency
  career academies and, 113
  core competencies, 7
  creative thinking, 54–55, 57–60, 115
  critical thinking, 8–9, 54–55, 61–63,
    115
  educational priorities, 6–8, 12–15
  financial literacy, 42–44, 115
  key capabilities, 8
  legal literacy, 44–46
  negotiation skills, 31–32, 46–47
  persuasion skills, 29–30
  powerful ideas, 8–11
  productive dialogue skills, 25–28
  resource management, 54–55, 66–67,
    115, 116
  survival skills, 7–8
  teamwork, 54–55, 67–69, 115
  time management, 54–55, 64–66, 116
  for tomorrow's workplace, 55–57, 69
Carnegie Commission, xiii
Carpenter, M. A., 65
Carr, N., 25
Case comparison
  in cost-benefit analysis, 62–63, 70,
    72, 74, 78, 95–96, 115–116
  as thinking skill, 52, 58
Casilli, C., 117
Causal and functional models, 93,
    96–98, 101
Causal chain analysis, 96
Central Park East Secondary School
    (Harlem, New York), 9–10, 14,
    105–107, 112, 117, 118
Central tendency measures, 85–86, 89
Charter schools, 106–107, 119–120
Chat rooms, 18, 22, 25
Check-ins, 65–66
Children's Machine, The (Papert), 10
China, 74, 79, 81
Cholesterol, 40
Christian, L., 38
Climate change, 75
Cline, H. F., 98
Club Penguin, 17

Cocking, R., 51–52
Cognitive apprenticeship, 109–110,
    113–114
Cohen, David K., 6–7, 8
Cohen, E. G., 68
Collaboration. *See* Teamwork
College loans, 44
Collins, Allan, xiii, 11, 18n1, 22–23,
    25n2, 28, 29, 32–33, 68, 84, 93,
    104, 110, 113
Command and Conquer (videogame),
    21
Communication skills, 9. *See also*
    Reading; Writing
  conflict management, 46, 47, 68
  negotiation, 31–32, 46–47
  persuasion, 29–30
  productive dialogue, 25–28
Community-of-learners model, 107–
    108, 111, 114–115
Competencies, 6–7, 8–9
Complexity. *See also* Public policy
  assessment and, 5–6
  education for complex society, 6–15
  globalization trend, ix, 79
  impact of, xiii–xv, 4, 13
  in mathematics, 4, 13
  need for teamwork, 70
  understanding complex systems,
    70–72
Computers. *See also* Internet; New
    literacy; Smartphones
  file organization, 66
  simulation and, 59–60, 110
Confirmatory investigations, 101–102
Conflict management, 46, 47, 68
Constraint systems, 98–99
Consumer Reports, 85
Conte, J. M., 65
Contracts, 44
Convincing arguments, 29
Cope, Edward, 46–47
Coppola, F. F., 1
Core competencies, 7
Correlation, 89–92
Cost-benefit analysis, 62–63, 70, 72,
    74, 78, 95–96, 115–116

Cover (Gentner), 57–58
Covert curriculum (Toffler), 3
Creative Attitude, The (Schank), 60
Creative thinking, 54–55, 57–60, 115
    in everyday life, 60
    examples of, 57–58
    strategies for, 58–60
Credit cards, 43
Cremin, L. A., xiv
Criminal law, 45
Crismond, D., 51, 109–110
Critical distinctions, 11
Critical-event analysis, 96
Critical factors, 59
Critical-incident analysis, 96
Critical thinking, 8–9, 54–55, 61–63,
    115
    evaluation skills in, 61–63
    strategies for, 62–63
Cross-functional teams, 67
Cross-product analysis, 96
Crowley, Chris, 37, 39–41
Cuban, L., 22
Cultural Literacy (Hirsch), xiii, 2, 4
Curriculum. *See* School curriculum
Cyberbullying, 25, 38, 45

Daiute, Colette, 19
Darling-Hammond, L., 9–10, 14, 106
Dawkins, R., 11
Deadlines, 38, 39, 49, 53, 64–66, 115
Debt
    credit cards, 43
    government, 77–78
    student loans, 44
Deep breathing, 38
Delayed gratification, 48–49, 65
Dementia, 40
Dependent variables, 87, 91
Depressions, 76–77
Design Club, 30, 31, 47
Devlin, Keith, 83, 92
Dewey, John, x
Dialogue skills, 25–28
Diaries, 109, 115
Diener, Edward, 47–48
Diet, 41–42, 102

Digital literacy, xiv, 23–25
Digital Youth Network, 14, 24–25, 33,
    66, 111, 112, 115, 117
Dinosaur curriculum, 112, 117
Discrimination, 45–46
Disney, 67
Dispositions, 9–10
Disruptive activities (Gentner), 57–58
Distributions, 88, 89
Diversity
    education of elites and nonelites,
        56–57
    equity issues for digital kids, 24,
        45–46, 56–57
    institutional racism, 45–46
Divorce, 32, 45
Domain frameworks, 11
Donnellon, Anne, 67–69
Dunbar, Kevin, 67
Dweck, Carol, 34, 50, 52, 65

Eastmond, E., 20, 115
Economic issues, 76–81
    economic cycles, 76–77
    globalization, 79
    government debt, 77–78
    growth rate of countries, 80–81
    incentives, 11, 78–79
    inflation, 76–77
    market function, 78
Edison, Thomas, 80
Ehrlich, Paul R., 73, 74
Einstein, Albert, 59–60, 92
Eisenhower, D. D., 49–50
Email, 18, 25, 64
Energy resources, 74
Environmental science, 72–75
    climate change, 75
    pollution, 74
    population growth, 72, 73
    resource depletion, 73–74
    species extinction, 75
Estimating skills, 13
Evaluation skills, 49–51, 61–63,
    102–103
Exercise, 39–41
Exploratory investigations, 101

Exponential growth, 87, 99, 100
Extinction, 75

Facebook, 17, 25, 38, 44, 64
Fadel, Charles, 8
Falk, B., 9–10, 14, 106
Fan fiction sites, 14, 17, 20, 33, 114
Fano, A., 110
Farming, 35, 56
Farrar, E., 6–7, 8
Fasse, B., 51, 109–110
Feedback in systems, 71
Ferguson, W., 93
Field view, 59
Film industry, 36
Financial advisors, 44
Financial crisis of 2008, 76–77
Financial literacy, 42–44, 115
Fisher, Roger, 31–32
*Five Elements of Effective Thinking,
  The* (Burger), 62–63
Fixed-intelligence mindset, 34
"Flat world" (Friedman), 56
Flynn, J. R., 2
Ford, Henry, 80
Foreign languages, 14
Form and function analysis, 97–98
Framingham Heart Study, 100–102
Franks, J. J., 52
Frederiksen, John R., 10, 26, 28, 32,
  47, 51, 61, 68, 93
Freelancing, 15, 35–36, 37, 42, 44–45,
  60
Friedman, Milton, 76
Friedman, Thomas L., 56
Functions, mathematical, 87–88
Future orientation, 65

Galileo, 86, 98–99, 101, 102
Gee, James Paul, 21, 25
Gentner, Dedre, 29, 57–60
Geographic information systems (GIS),
  110
Geography, 12
Getting to Yes (Fisher et al.), 31–32
Gibson, C. B., 65
"Gig economy," 15, 35–36, 37, 42,
  44–45, 60

Global Achievement Gap, The
  (Wagner), 7–8, 83–84
Globalization
  education for, 81–82
  growth rate of countries, 80–81
  mathematics in, 83–84
  trend toward, ix, 79
Globaloria, 23–25, 33, 111
Goal-based scenarios, 110
Gomez, K., 14, 24, 112
Google, 66, 107
Government, 12–13, 77–78. *See also*
  Public policy
Graduation requirements, 14–15, 105–
  106, 117, 118–119
Graham, J., 38
Graphs, 86–87, 102–103
Gray, J., 51, 109–110
Great Britain
  Industrial Revolution, 56, 74, 80,
    84, 92
  prisoners on ships to Australia, 11, 78
Great Depression, 76, 77
Green Eggs and Ham (Dr. Seuss), 23
Green Revolution, 73
Growth mindset, 34, 50, 52
Guise, S., 65
Gurian, P., 1

Habitat for Humanity, 43
Habits of Mind, 9–10, 105–106
Halpern, Diane F., 62, 63
Halverson, E. Richard, xiii, 18n1, 22–
  23, 32–33, 104, 110–111
Hammer, M., 61
Hardin, Garret, 71, 73–74
Hatano, Giyoo, 51
Hawke, Ethan, 36
Health-care costs, 78–79
Healthy lifestyle, 37–42, 115
  exercise, 39–41
  nutritious diet, 41–42, 102
  risky behavior versus, 37, 39, 41
  stress management, 37–39, 40
Heart disease, 38–39, 40, 100–102
Heath, S. B., 19, 62
Helm, Judy Harris, 111–112
Hershman, L. W., 61

Hickey, D. T., 117
Hiebert, J., 52
Hierarchy analysis, 95–96
High School II (Wiseman), 105
High Tech Schools (San Diego area),
    106–107, 119
Hirsch, E. D., Jr., xiii, 2, 4
History, 12
Hmelo-Silver, C. E., 72, 109
Hoadley, C. M., 25
Holbrook, J., 51, 109–110
Holum, A., 110
Home ownership, 43–44
Home Shopping Network, 49
Hsi, S., 25
Hypotheses, 99–101

IBM, Watson, 55, 84
Impulse control, 48–49
Inagaki, Kayoko, 51
Incentives, 11, 78–79
Independent variables, 87, 91
India, 74, 81
Industrial Revolution, 56, 74, 80, 84, 92
Inferences, statistical, 90–92
Inflation, 76–77
Innovation
    in school curriculum, 108–111,
        114–117
    technological, 80–81
Institutional racism, 45–46
Interest groups, and school curriculum,
    2–3
Interesting arguments, 29–30
Intermediate constructs (Gentner),
    57–58
Internet, 4
    arts and, 14
    chat rooms, 18, 22, 25
    cyberbullying, 25, 38, 45
    fan fiction sites, 14, 17, 20, 33, 114
    fostering literacy for all, 22–25
    impact on education, 12, 14, 18–22,
        84
    social media, 17, 25, 38, 44, 45, 64
    virtual worlds, 19, 21, 28
Introduction to Mathematical Thinking
    (Devlin), 83, 92

Investigative skills, 9
    collecting information, 26–28, 52
    contrasting cases, 52, 58
    designing scientific investigations,
        101–102
    in science, 99–103
    Web of Inquiry, 26–28
IQ tests, 2, 49, 60

Japan, 80–81
Jefferson, Thomas, xiv, 2, 4, 71
Jenkins, Henry, 25
Jennings, Ken, 55
Jeopardy! (TV game show), 55
Jobs, Steve, 14
Johnson, Steven, 54
Jona, M., 110
Joseph, Diana, 113–114, 117–118
Jung, Yan, 30

Kafai, Y. B., 20, 110–111, 115
Kapur, M., 52, 68
Kiecolt-Glaser, J., 38
Knobel, Michele, 21
Kolodner, Janet L., 51, 109–110, 116
Konnikova, M., 48

Laina, V., 117
Law
    automation in, 56
    legal literacy, 44–46, 115
Law of supply and demand, 78
Leadership skills, 21, 30, 56–57, 65–66,
    69, 71, 76
Leading indicators, 99, 100
Leander, Kevin, 21
Learning by Design, 109–110, 115
Lego Mindstorms, 112
LEGO models, 30
Lehrer, J., 48
Lehrer, R., 86–87
Leu, Don J., 21
Leverage point, 71
Lewis, Cynthia, 17
Lifelong learning, ix, 4, 8, 106, 111
Linear functions, 87
Line graphs, 86
Lippert, M., 40

Lodge, Henry S., 37, 39–41
Looking for Data in All the Right Places (Starko & Schack), 116–117
Lowell, Francis Cabot, 80

Maker movement, 110–111
Maloney, J., 20, 115
Mandinach, E. B., 98
Mangiola, L., 19, 62
Markets, 78
Markoff, J., 55
Marsh, O. C., 46–47
Marshmallow experiment, 48
Martin, C., 14, 24, 112
Martin, Odile, 54
Massachusetts Institute of Technology (MIT), 80, 87–88
Mass Effect (videogame), 21
Massively multiplayer online games (MMOGs), 21
Mathematics, 85–92, 116–117
    computers in, 4, 13
    correlation, 89–92
    critical skills in, 103
    functions, 87–88
    global importance of, 83–84
    graphs, 86–87, 102–103
    inferences from statistics, 90–92
    international comparisons of student performance, 3
    mathematizing situations, 84–86, 92, 117
    problem types, 13
    relevance of, 1, 13, 14
    rethinking curriculum, 84–85
    statistics, 88–92
    teaching to learn, 62–63
    teamwork in, 50–51
    variables, 85–86, 87, 89–92
McAfee, Andrew, 55
McDonald's, 44–45
Meadows, Donnella H., 70–72, 98
Mean, 85–86
Median, 85–86, 89
Medicine
    computers in medical diagnosis, 55, 84

hormone replacement therapy (HRT), 90
    inferences on drug effectiveness, 90–91
    problem-based learning in, 108–109
Meditation, 38
Meier, Deborah, 9–10, 105
Memorable arguments, 30
Mentoring, x, 16, 19, 24, 47, 63, 105, 107, 114–115, 119
Mexico, 79
Michaels, S., 26, 28
Millner, A., 20, 115
Mindset (Dweck), 34
Mindstorms (Papert), 4
Minecraft, 30
Mischel, Walter, 46, 48
MMOGs (massively multiplayer online games), 21
Mode, 85–86
Modeling strategies, 93
Model types
    behavioral, 94, 98–99, 101
    causal and functional, 93, 96–98, 101
    structural, 93, 94–96, 101
Modularity, 10–11
Monitoring skills, 49–51
Monroy-Hernández, A., 20, 115
Moose Crossing, 19, 28
Multifactor analysis, 97
Multitasking, 64–65
Multi-user virtual environments (MUVEs), 19
Music, 88, 91–92
MUVEs (multi-user virtual environments), 19

Nass, Clifford, 64–65
National Heart, Lung, and Blood Institute, 41
Near-misses, 58–59
Neary, L., 23
Negotiation skills, 31–32
    interests versus positions, 31–32
    objective criteria in resolving differences, 32

options for mutual gain, 32
relationship issues and, 46, 47, 68
separating people from problem, 31
situation awareness, 46–47
teamwork and, 46, 47, 69
NetLogo, 98, 103, 118
Networked digital media, 21–22
Neville, P., 29
Newell, A., 99
New Literacies Sampler, A (Lewis), 17
New literacy, 17–33
    basic versus applied literacies and,
        17–18
    changing face of literacy, 18–22
    core literacy versus, 17, 18, 20–22,
        24
    literacy for all, 22–25, 32–33
    negotiation skills, 31–32
    persuasion skills, 29–30
    productive dialogue, 25–28
Newman, S. E., 110
Newton, Isaac, 87, 92
New York School of the Performing
    Arts, 113
Nintendo DS game system, 23
Normal distribution, 88, 89
Northwestern University, 6–7, 8–9
Nutrition, 41–42, 102

Obama, Barack, ix
Obama, Michelle, 41
Obesity, 39, 41, 79
Objective criteria, 32
O'Byrne, W. I., 117
O'Connor, C., 26, 28
Ophir, Eyal, 64–65
Overtones, 88

Packer, A., 1–2
Papert, Seymour, 4–5, 10
Parents
    in community-of-learners model,
        107–108
    demand for charter schools, 120
    and "passion schools," 111
Park, A., 41
Particle view, 59

Participatory cultures (Jenkins), 25
Passion schools, 104–120
    assessment practices, 117–119
    community of learners and, 114–115
    curricular innovations, 108–111,
        114–117
    elements of, 105–111
    goal of, 117
    nature of, 104–105, 111
    new school designs, 105–108,
        111–114
    as schools of the future, 119–120
    vision for restructuring schools, 104,
        111–119
Patton, Bruce, 31–32
PBL (problem-based learning), 108–
    109, 110, 115, 116
Peer teaching, x, 16, 62–63, 105
Peggy Sue Got Married (movie), 1, 13,
    14
Pepper, C., 38
Peppler, K., 110–111
Perfectionism, 65
Perspective shifts, 59
Persuasion skills, 29–30
Philadelphia Museum of Natural
    History, 46
Pie charts, 86
Piety, Philip J., 5
Pike, Kenneth L., 58, 59
Pinkard, N., 14, 24, 112
Planning skills, 49–51, 65–66
Poe, M. T., 29
Poisson distribution, 88
Pollan, M., 41
Pollution, 74
Population Bomb (Ehrlich), 73, 74
Population growth, 72–74
Portfolios, 66, 105–107, 116–118
Positive feedback loop, 71
Postman, Neil, 15
Powell, A. G., 6–7, 8
Power issues, 47, 68
Power law, 88–89
Power of Their Ideas, The (Meier), 105
Problem-based learning (PBL), 108–
    109, 110, 115, 116

Problem-centered analysis, 96–97
Procrastination, 65
Productive dialogue, 25–28
Productive thinking
   creative, 54–56, 57–60, 115
   critical thinking, 54–55, 61–63, 115
Progressive relaxation, 38
Project-Based Inquiry Science (Kolodner
   et al.), 109
Public policy, xiv, 12–13, 70–82
   addressing societal problems, 70,
     71–72, 81–82
   complex systems and, 70–72
   economic issues, 76–81
   environmental issues, 72–75
   government debt, 77–78
   teamwork and, 72
   tragedy of the commons (Hardin),
     71, 73–74
Publishing industry, 56
Puntambekar, S., 51, 109–110

Racism, 45–46
Randomized trials, 90, 102
Reading
   fan fiction sites, 14, 17, 20, 33, 114
   handheld devices and, 23
   literary canon, 13–14, 23, 56
   student interests and, 13–14
   texting and, 15, 17, 22, 25–26, 64
Reflective practice, x, 49–51, 66
Reisman, K., 60, 98
Relationships. See also Teamwork
   conflict management, 46, 47, 68
   divorce and, 32, 45
   power issues, 47, 68
   situation awareness in, 46–47
Relaxation, 38
Remix World, 24
Research questions, 99–101
Resnick, L. B., 26, 28
Resnick, Mitchel, 20, 98, 115
Resource depletion, 73–74
Resource management, 54–55, 66–67,
   115, 116
Rethinking Education in the Age of
   Technology (Collins & Halverson),
   32–33, 104

Reverse Heart Disease Now (Sinatra &
   Roberts), 38–39
Rewired (Rosen), 64
Rhetoric (Young et al.), 58, 59
Risky behavior, 37, 39, 41
Roberts, James C., 38–39
Robinson, Ken, 60
Robots, 54, 55
Rogoff, Barbara, 107–108, 111, 115,
   119
Rosen, Larry D., 64
Rosenbaum, E., 20, 115
Rubrics, 5, 105, 118
Rumsfeld, Donald, 52
Rusk, N., 20, 115
Rutter, Brad, 55
Ryan, M., 51, 109–110

Sadler, Philip M., 1
SAT, 48, 49, 118
Satisficing (Simon), 65
Savings accounts, 42–43
Saxenian, A., 80
SCANS Commission, 7, 67
Scatter plots, 86
Schack, Gina D., 116–117
Schank, Roger C., 60, 110
Schauble, L., 86–87
Schedules, 66–67
Schenke, K., 117
Schmidt, William H., 3
Schoenfeld, Alan J., 50–51
School curriculum
   assessment and. See Assessment
   dispositions, 105–107
   educational priorities, 6–8, 12–15
   inclusion of topics, 2–3
   influence of testing on, 4–6
   inheritance from the past, 3–4
   innovations in, 108–111, 114–117
   interest groups and, 2–3
   powerful ideas in, 8–11
   relevance of information, 1–6
   what is worth learning, 12–15
School design, 105–108, 111–114
Schwartz, A. J., 76
Science, 92–103, 116–117
   critical skills in, 103

data analysis and synthesis, 102–103
environmental issues, 72–75
international comparisons of student
    performance, 3
models, 93–99
problem types, 13
research design, 101–102
research questions and hypotheses,
    99–101
rethinking curriculum, 84–85
scientific inquiry cycle, 92–93
teamwork in, 67
Sciences of the Artificial, The (Simon),
    10–11
Scratch community, 20, 33, 115
Second Machine Age, The (Brynjolfsson
    & McAfee), 55
Secretary's Commission on Achieving
    Necessary Skills (SCANS), 7, 67
Self-control, 47–49, 115
Selfridge, Oliver, 58, 60
Self-sufficiency, 34–53, 115
    adaptive expertise, 9, 51–52
    financial literacy, 42–44, 115
    freelancing, 15, 35–36, 37, 42,
        44–45, 60
    growing need for self-reliance, 35–36
    growth mindset and, 34, 50, 52
    healthy lifestyle, 37–42, 115
    improving self-control, 47–49, 115
    legal literacy, 44–46, 115
    monitoring skills, 49–51
    planning skills, 49–51, 65–66
    reflecting skills, 49–51
    schooling for self-reliance, 53
    strategic relationships, 46–47
Seligman, Martin E. P., 48
Seymour (movie), 36
Shaffer, David W., 110, 112–114
Shakespeare, William, 13–14, 56,
    94–95
Sherwood, R. D., 52
Shimoda, T., 30, 47
Silicon Valley, 80
Silver, J., 20, 115
Silverman, B., 20, 115
Simon, Herbert A., 10–11, 65, 99
Simon, Julian L., 73, 74

Simulation, 59–60, 110
Sinatra, Stephen T., 38–39
Sine function, 88
Sine waves, 88
Situation-action models, 99
Situation awareness, 46–47
Six sigma, 88
Slope, 87
Smartphones
    reading and, 23
    scheduling with, 66–67
    translations and, 14
Smith, Adam, 71
Social media, 17, 25, 38, 44, 45, 64
Social networking sites, 18–19
South Korea, 81
Spatial decomposition models, 94
Stage models, 94–95
Stager, C., 75
Stanford University, 80
Starbird, Michael, 62
Starko, Alane J., 116–117
Star Wars: Galaxies (videogame), 21
Statistics, 88–92
    central tendency measures, 85–86, 89
    correlation, 89–92
    distributions, 88, 89
    inferences in, 90–92
STEM disciplines, 84–85. *See also*
    Mathematics; Science
Sticks and Stones (Bazelon), 45
Stigler, J., 52
Strategic approach
    adaptive expertise, 9, 51–52
    for being persuasive, 29–30
    for creative thinking, 58–60
    for critical thinking, 62–63
    modeling, 93
    planning and, 49–51, 65–66
    situation awareness, 46–47
    strategic mindset and, 34–35
    strategic relationships, 46–47
    for successful living, 10
    for time management, 65–67
Stress management, 37–39, 40
Structural models, 93, 94–96, 101
Student loans, 44
Substantive arguments, 29

Summit Public Schools, 107, 119
Sunk costs, 43

Taiwan, 81
Tamblyn, R. M., 72, 108–109
Target structure, 60
Tarnier, Stephane, 54
Teamwork, 54–55, 67–69, 115
   in brainstorming, 32
   complexity and, 70–72
   cross-functional teams, 67
   key success issues, 68–69
   in mathematics, 50–51
   negotiation skills and, 46, 47, 69
   public policy issues and, 72
   in science, 67
Temporal decomposition models, 94–95
Testing, 4–6, 41, 118–119
   IQ tests, 2, 49, 60
   SAT, 48, 49, 118
Texting, 15, 17, 22, 25–26, 64
Thinking in Systems (Meadows),
   70–72, 98
Third International Mathematics and
   Science Study (TIMSS), 3
Thomas, Douglas, 21
Tierney, John, 48–49, 65
Time management, 54–55, 64–66, 116
   deadlines, 38, 39, 49, 53, 64–66, 115
   multitasking, 64–65
   procrastination, 65
   schedules, 66–67
   strategies for, 65–67
TinkerPlots, 86–87, 103
Toffler, Alvin, 3
Too Big to Know (Weinberger), ix
Toprani, D., 30, 47
Tort law, 44–45
Tragedy of the commons (Hardin), 71,
   73–74
Tree-structure analysis, 95–96
Trend analysis, 99, 100
Trilling, Bernie, 8
Turkle, Sherry, 25, 26
21st Century Skills (Trilling & Fadel), 8
Twitter, 25
Tyagi, Amelia Warren, 42–43

"Über generation," 35–36, 37, 42,
   44–45, 60
Understandable arguments, 30
Uniform distribution, 88
Universal schooling model, 3
Ury, William, 31–32
U.S. Department of Labor, 7, 67

Valverde, Gilbert A., 3
Variables, 85–86, 89–92
   correlation, 89–92
   dependent, 87, 91
   independent, 87, 91
   inferences concerning, 90–92
Vehicles in Motion unit, 109–110
Videogames, 19, 20–21, 23, 24, 28,
   39, 41
Virtual worlds, 19, 21, 28
Visualization, 38
Vye, N. J., 52

Wagner, Anthony, 7–8, 64–65, 83–84
Waller, M. J., 65
Wall Street Journal, 54
Warren, Elizabeth, 42–43
Washington, George, xiv, 71
Water resources, 73–74
Watson (IBM), 55, 84
Wave view, 59
Web communities, 17, 20
Webkinz World, 17
Web of Inquiry, 26–28
Weinberg, Sam, 2
Weinberger, David, ix
Where Good Ideas Come From
   (Johnson), 54
White, Barbara Y., 10, 25n2, 26, 28,
   32, 47, 51, 61, 68, 91–92, 93,
   116
Whiteboards, 32, 108, 110, 115
Wikipedia, 11, 44, 55
Wilensky, U., 60, 98
Wilkerson-Jerde, Michelle, 117
Willis, J. E., 117
Willpower, 48–49, 65
Willpower (Baumeister & Tierney),
   48–49, 65

Wilson, E. O., 75
Wiseman, Frederick, 105
Within-subject variables, 91
Workplace skills. *See* Career skills
Writing
   assessing, 5
   fan fiction sites, 14, 17, 20, 33, 114
   self-publishing trend, 56
   texting and, 15, 17, 22, 25–26, 64
Wythe, George, xiv

Xanga, 20
Xerox, 67

Yan, S., 30, 47
Y-intercept, 87
Young, Richard E., 58, 59
Younger Next Year (Crowley & Lodge), 37

Zumbrum, J., 54

About the Author

Allan Collins is professor emeritus of learning sciences at Northwestern University. He is a member of the National Academy of Education and has been elected a fellow of the American Association for Artificial Intelligence, the Cognitive Science Society, the American Association for the Advancement of Science, and the American Educational Research Association. He served as a founding editor of the journal *Cognitive Science* and as first chair of the Cognitive Science Society. He is best known in psychology for his work on semantic memory and mental models, in artificial intelligence for his work on plausible reasoning and intelligent tutoring systems, and in education for his work on inquiry teaching, cognitive apprenticeship, situated learning, design research, epistemic forms and games, and systemic validity in educational testing. From 1991 to 1994, he was codirector of the U.S. Department of Education's Center for Technology in Education. His book with Richard Halverson, *Rethinking Education in the Age of Technology: The Digital Revolution and Schooling in America*, was published by Teachers College Press in September 2009.